TOMMY

DOUGHBOY

FRITZ

SOLDIER SLANG
OF WORLD WAR I

TOMMY

DOUGHBOY

FRITZ

SOLDIER SLANG OF WORLD WAR I

EMILY BREWER

AMBERLEY

First published 2014

Amberley Publishing
The Hill, Stroud
Gloucestershire, GL5 4EP

www.amberley-books.com

British Library Cataloguing in Publication Data.
A catalogue record for this book is available from the British Library.

ISBN 978 1 4456 3783 9

Typeset in 11.5pt on 12pt Sabon.
Typesetting and Origination by Amberley Publishing.
Printed in the UK.

Contents

Acknowledgements   7

Introduction   9

Tommy   17

Doughboy   107

Fritz   183

Bibliography   215

Acknowledgements

Throughout the process of writing this book, I have been continually amazed by the kindness and willingness to help shown to me by academics and interested parties. In particular, I would like to thank Tim Cook, Jonathon Green and Tony Thorne.

Credit is also due to many archives around the world, who have preserved war diaries, trench newspapers and letters, digitised them, and uploaded them to the Internet. Without them, our view of the realities of everyday life in the trenches would be nowhere near as extensive as it is now.

Introduction

The First World War, the Great War, the War to End all Wars – the conflict between 1914 and 1918 has been known by many names, and words have always been an important part of its legacy. Now that one hundred years have passed since the beginning of the war, the contributions of the 65 million men who were actively involved in the fighting are bound to be brought sharply into focus, and rightly so. Around 9.5 million men died over the course of the war, and all mobilised soldiers experienced hardship, heartache and heroism in circumstances that are unimaginable to those of us who have never seen fighting on such a large scale.

For the First World War truly was a global one. Although much of the action took place in Europe, soldiers from all six inhabited continents played their parts. These men faced enormous difficulties and privations on the front line, and it is easy to forget, in our much smaller world of cheap airfares and regular travel, that many of them were travelling to different countries for the first time. They were meeting new people and learning new languages – on paper, it sounds very exciting, but it was no holiday.

All of this influenced soldiers' slang, which quickly became another language to learn. It was made up of dialect, archaic terms, rhyming slang, puns, foreign words and neologisms, and was quickly adopted as a common ground for communication. It was discussed in newspapers, both trench and civilian, and soldiers wrote home about it, sometimes using it in their writing. Some people felt it was damaging existing languages, and others embraced it as a natural evolution; regardless, in many cases, it has remained a part of our vocabulary.

Much has been written on the purpose and use of slang. It can be used as a way of defining a group – if you understand the lingo, you're part of the club. We see this use of slang commonly in teenagers. The use of language is different dependent on age, and so we have such examples as 'sick' – meaning either 'ill' or 'good', depending on one's background and generation. This 'one of the gang' function is an important aspect of trench slang; many of the soldiers were away from all their friends and family, so feeling like part of a community would be very useful in coping and coming to terms with the situation.

Naturally, if understanding the slang can ingratiate you into a group, being unfamiliar with it can also exclude you. Anyone who has sat alone in a rural village pub listening to the locals' dialect knows this. Soldiers were proud of their secret language; speaking fluent trench slang set them apart from civilians – they had seen and lived through things that those back home could not possibly hope to comprehend. The troops did not want outsiders to understand their language; it belonged to those at the front and no one else. It also served as useful marker of differing ranks within the Army. Officers were not 'one of us', and so the slang was not theirs, either.

On a purely practical level, words had to be invented to explain new situations and experiences; it was the only way of describing events that had never before been seen. In addition to this, language became a coping mechanism – trivialisation of the horror witnessed on a daily basis was necessary for maintaining morale. Psychologically, making a joke out of a terrifying prospect can do much to remove the fear and threat felt by those who face it.

The soldiers also had to deal with unfamiliar people and places. Much soldier slang involved the ironic mispronunciation of foreign words (this was particularly the case with French words among the British troops), or the transfer of words from other languages or cultures into common parlance. These were times and circumstances in which men from vastly different backgrounds were thrown together, and it was vital that they found common ground in order to work well as a unit. Thus, we find several words from Hindi that became equally common alternatives to their English counterparts.

The influence of trench slang did not stop on the front line, however. With such large numbers of men being mobilised over the four years of the war, it was inevitable that at least some of the language would make it back home. When researching this book, I was amazed at the number of terms that originated, or experienced a resurgence, in the trenches, and yet are still used; this was common to French and English. Of course, some words were very much of their time, and would not make the transition into everyday use, so they have now become historical artefacts.

To reflect the sacrifices made by soldiers from all over the world, with such differing linguistic heritage, I have endeavoured to include soldier slang from other languages. Often, this proved difficult, so many languages are still not represented here. There is not much scholarship on the subject of soldier slang in certain countries. As a linguist, I found this very interesting – is slang a phenomenon limited to specific cultures?

It is worth noting at this point that many archaic words enjoyed something of a resurgence during the First World War, taking on new meanings or simply re-entering popular language. Similarly, some dialect passed from very localised into national usage. This highlights the fact that people from all over were mixing, and sharing their linguistic tendencies. I have included examples of both ancient words and regional vocabulary, since both form part of the rich tapestry of trench language.

It has been interesting to research slang in various languages, as many of the terms are similar. All languages seem to have nicknames for weapons and death; all have words originating in dialect; all include references to the different ranks in the army. It is easy to forget, in the midst of arguments over right and wrong, that many of the soldiers on both sides were ordinary men, fighting on behalf of someone else. They suffered similar hardship, got through it in the same way – particularly with humour – and ultimately understood each other. Testament to this is the well-documented Christmas truce of 1914.

The book is divided into three sections: Tommy (looking at slang from all over the Commonwealth), Doughboy (including slang from the other Entente Powers), and Fritz (a collection of German and Austrian slang). I hope that you enjoy it, and find it both interesting and informative. Of all the things for which we have to thank the soldiers of the First World War, language may seem unimportant, but I see it as a small, everyday kind of tribute, ensuring that we will never forget them.

Tommy

This section looks at the slang used and invented by the Commonwealth soldiers. Tommy, of course, refers to the British soldier, but ours were not the only Commonwealth men in the war.

Canada and Newfoundland (which was a separate territory at this time) sent 600,000 and 12,000 men respectively to Europe to help with the war effort. Because Canada sent an initial contingent of 25,000 soldiers in 1914, there was much intermingling with the British forces, and so many of the slang words were common to both groups. In these instances, it is difficult to determine where the phrase originated. I have included entries based on the sources I used to find them.

Around 800,000 Indian soldiers served in the First World War, mostly from Punjab. Unfortunately, there has been no research into the use of slang among these soldiers, potentially because they were fighting with British men, and thus spoke English. Nevertheless, Hindi, in particular, was integrated into soldier slang, and thus the Indian nation is represented here through borrowings.

Conversely, among the Australian troops and those from New Zealand, slang played a very important role, and its use has been extensively documented. The word 'digger' was used by both the Australian and the New Zealand forces to mean friend, and became so common that the slang spoken by these men has been christened Digger speak. 'Digger' speak certainly seems to have been a distinct and separate 'slanguage', although, as is to be expected, it also incorporated slang from other nationalities. Perhaps this distinctiveness can be attributed to the initial Australasian wartime experience; most were posted to Gallipoli and the Middle East, particularly in the early years of the war, and so their experiences must necessarily have been different.

Tommy, the term used for a British soldier, came from the example used by the Army on recruitment forms, which had the name Tommy Atkins written on them when demonstrating how to fill them in. Tommies were also known as Woodbines and Limeys.

~

A fair whack – in the trenches, there was a very strong feeling of camaraderie and community, so when someone received a parcel, it was common for them to share out the contents: they would 'whack' it around equally. It has been suggested that 'whack' meant to divide (perhaps as a result of being hit) as early as 1785. *'You've had more than a fair whack.'*

A1 – before men could be accepted into the Army, they had to be tested for general fitness. The scale went from A1 to C3, A1 being excellent, and C3 completely unfit for service overseas. This use transferred to mean 'happy' or 'on excellent form'. A similar classification system was used for ships in the Lloyd's Register, which was founded in the mid-eighteenth century, so it is possible that this gave the Army the idea. *'I hope you're well; I'm A1.'*

Abdominal – a nicer version of gutzer, meaning a crash. This was used across the forces, whereas gutzer tended to be used mostly by the Australian troops.

Abdul – a term used to refer to Turkish soldiers. This seems to have been used mostly by the Australian forces; many of their battles were against the Turks in Egypt.

A Canada – a Canadian term denoting a wound bad enough to warrant being sent back to Canada. For some, this would be seen as a blessing in disguise, but the wound would have had to be extremely serious for such a drastic measure to be taken. *'If he has lost both arms and both legs, and both eyes shot out, one ear off and part of his nose, he might get "a Canada".'*

Ack-Ack – this was a popular implementation of 'Signalese', the phonetic alphabet used by signallers in the First World War. 'Ack' was the representation for the letter 'A', so Ack-Ack meant AA, which stood for anti-aircraft fire. Signalese was used quite extensively in the trenches; other examples include Emma-Pip (MP), which meant a military policeman. *'The Ack-Acks were being used all night.'*

Ack-Emma – as above, from Signalese. 'Emma' was the representation for the letter 'M', so Ack-Emma meant 'AM'. It was used either as 'in the morning' or to refer to an air mechanic. *'It's 3.50 ack emma.'*

Ak dum – meaning immediately. This is one of the many Hindi words used as English slang, perhaps because there had already been much interaction overseas between British soldiers and Indians.

Alley at the toot – here is an example of a mispronunciation of the French, *allez tout de suite* ('go straightaway'). It was one of many such examples in the odd mix of French and English that soldiers spoke.

Alleyman – this came from a mispronunciation of the French word *allemand*, which meant German (or perhaps *Allemagne*, meaning Germany). It was one of many names for the German soldiers used by the Entente Powers, and was used in a trench song called 'I Want to Go Home':

I want to go home, I want to go home.
I don't want to go in the trenches no more,
Where whizzbangs and shrapnel they whistle and
roar.

Take me over the sea, where the Alleyman can't get at me.

Oh my, I don't want to die,

I want to go home.

Andy McNoon – an idiot. This was most popular with Australian troops, perhaps as a result of their exposure to Arabic while in Egypt, as 'inta machnoon' is supposed to mean a damned fool. An unqualified idiot. From the Arabic تنأ نونجم, pronounced 'enet majnoon', which means 'you madman'.

Antonio – this, among other nicknames, was used when referring to Portuguese soldiers (specifically, privates). Sometimes it was shortened to Tony. There were nicknames for most of the participants in the war.

Anzac soup – water in a shell hole that had been turned foul by a corpse. This was a particular problem for the Australian troops, who spent much time in Africa, as the heat meant that water was a valuable commodity, but quickly went putrid.

Anzac stew – Army stew diluted down more than was usual. This meal was supposedly made with hot water and a bacon rind.

Anzac wafer – these were common in Africa, and were the standard Army biscuits. They were supposedly very hard, and apparently unappetising. *'All we had to eat was bully and Anzac wafers.'*

Argue the toss – still commonly used today, this expression means to have an argument. It seems to come from flipping a coin and, given the prevalence and popularity of card games in the trenches, it would make sense that the phrase started in relation to gambling.

Army rocks – rhyming slang, meaning 'socks'. This term is only documented in *The Long Trail* by Brophy and Partridge, and no explanation is given. Perhaps socks were given this name because they were uncomfortable, or maybe it just rhymed conveniently. Among the British and Australian troops, rhyming slang was common.

Arrival – referred to a shell bursting behind British lines. This is an instance of trivialising what could otherwise be a frightening situation.

Arsapeek – upside down. This seems to have been used primarily by Australian troops.

Arse-ups – the nickname of the 4th New Zealand Rifle Brigade, apparently because of the shape of their shoulder badges.

Arsty – another example of the use of Hindi terms within British slang. This was a corrupted version of आहिस्ता, pronounced 'ahista', which means slowly.

Atcha – used to mean yes, the word actually comes from the Hindi for good, अच्छा, using the same pronunciation (which is rather unusual; more often than not, pronunciation changed slightly, as in 'arsty', above).

Attaboy – there is some debate over the original meaning of this word, but it was popularised during the First World War. Some have suggested that it is a bastardised version of 'that's a boy!'

Baby elephant – this was the Australian nickname for one of the scout aeroplanes frequently flown in Egypt.

Baby's head – this was a meat pudding, one of the staple Army rations. It was made with meat, flour, suet, onion, baking powder, pepper and salt. Food was a rich source of slang, and there are several uncomplimentary references to how it tasted or looked. *'I could just eat a baby's head.'*

Back curtain – when troops were going out on a raid, they referred to it as a show, so this could be a continuation of the trivialisation theme. Alternatively, it could simply describe the act; a back curtain involved raining artillery fire down behind the German line to prevent them from bringing in reinforcements, creating a curtain of fire at the back of the Germans.

Backchat – from the Hindi बातचीत, pronounced 'batchit', which means conversation. Its use developed into the modern-day word during the First World War, as it took on the meaning of jokey banter.

Badmash – from the Hindi बदमाश, with the same pronunciation. This word was used to mean a scoundrel or rascal, and is yet another example of the Indian influence on trench slang.

Bag of rations – this was a scathing reference to someone who was overenthusiastic. In another example of the divide between Tommies and the higher-ranking soldiers, this was often used in reference to superiors.

Balloon buster – the nickname used for a pilot who was particularly good at shooting down observation balloons. The best balloon buster of the war was Willy Coppens, a Belgian; he shot down thirty-seven balloons over his career.

Banjo – an Australianism meaning shovel. It is thought that the name derives from the similar shape.

Barker – slang both for pistols and sausages, the latter because some soldiers suggested dog meat was involved.

Base case – a wound severe enough to be sent back to base to rest, but not bad enough to be sent back home.

Base rat – a soldier who stayed in the rear and somehow never made it to the front.

Bat – another word that comes from Hindi. It means language, and was commonly used in the expression 'swing the bat', which meant that you spoke the local language.

Battle bowler – officer slang for the manganese steel Brodie helmet. This is a good example of differences in ranks in terms of slang, as the average Tommy would simply have referred to the helmet as a tin hat or tin jug.

Be knocked out – to die, in Canadian troop slang. With the prospect of death all around these soldiers, their usual coping mechanism was to diminish it or to refer to it in obscure terms.

Become a landowner – this was another expression meaning to die. The implication was that you would own the land you were buried in.

Behind the lines – a self-explanatory phrase still in use today. It is surprising how many words whose origins lie in the First World War are used everyday in modern English. *'I travelled to a town 2 miles behind the lines.'*

Belgie – a Belgian. The origin of the word is obvious, and is surprisingly uninventive given the wealth of creative references to other nationalities.

Belgique – comes from the French adjective, meaning Belgian. In the First World War, it was used by English-speaking troops as an adjective meaning odd or unusual.

Bert – an ironic reference to the French town of Albert. There were several such anglicised names for towns on the front, many of which were pronounced incorrectly on purpose.

Bill Adams/Sweet Fanny Adams – bugger all/ sweet f*%k all. There was quite a culture of swearing in the forces at this time, although this offended some of the milder-mannered men; perhaps this is why phrases like this were invented. *'There is Bill Adams.'*

Binge – authors Doyle and Walker claimed in their book that this was popularised during the war to describe drinking too much alcohol. It had previously been used only regionally, supposedly either in Lancashire or in Lincolnshire, where it was used in the sense 'to soak' during the mid-nineteenth century.

Biscuits – unfortunately not the sweet kind. The term referred to small Army mattresses, which were apparently very hard.

Black Hand Gang – referred to a group of soldiers who were going on a raid or a difficult mission with a strong element of danger. The phrase is said to come from the Black Hand movement in Serbia, whose assassination of

Archduke Franz Ferdinand was one of the causes of the First World War.

Blanket drill – this referred to the practice by some soldiers of having a nap in the afternoon (it tended to be soldiers who had served in India or Africa, and had become accustomed to sleeping in the afternoon heat). A second meaning was masturbation.

Blighty – the term is said to come from the Hindi for foreign, which was pronounced bilayati or vilayati. It was brought back by British troops who had been posted in India – as they were always referred to this way, they began to associate it with home and corrupted the term into an anglicised form.

Oh, jam for tea! Oh, jam for tea!
Fried bully and maconochie;
But when we get back to Blighty-y-y
We will have ham and lamb for tea.

Blighty one/Blighty wound/A Blighty – a wound severe enough to get the soldier sent back home. Self-inflicted blighty wounds were a capital offense. Though none were executed, nearly 4,000 men were convicted of self-inflicted wounds and were sent to prison. *'He was lucky enough to receive a blighty wound.'*

Blind pig – one of the many names for a German mortar bomb. This slang was used most commonly by the Canadian troops.

Blitherer – an Australianism, meaning something or someone excellent. Given that blithered meant drunk, perhaps this term developed from someone who was the life and soul of the party when drunk, or from a particularly strong drink that inebriated anyone who imbibed it.

Blood's worth bottling – another example of Digger speak, meaning that someone was worth their salt.

Blotto – meaning drunk. There have been several discussions about the origin of the word. It might come from blotting paper, which soaks up liquid. The author Albert Jack, however, claims that it came into existence because of some notoriously unstable bicycles manufactured by Blotto Frères of Paris and used on the front – they had difficulty staying upright, in the same way as a drunkard might. *'He's completely blotto.'*

Bludged on the flag – 'to bludge' was an Australianism meaning to impose upon someone. It was adapted during the war to refer to an incompetent soldier.

Blue duck – this is one of the rare examples I have been able to find of slang specific to New Zealand soldiers. It meant an unfounded rumour, presumably because there's no such thing as a blue duck.

Blue lamp – a brothel catering only to officers. There were over 100 'knocking shops', as they were also known, in the towns near the front line.

Bluff stakes – an attempt to influence someone in a deceitful way. This expression appears to only have been used by the Australians. *'I tried to put on the bluff stakes but it didn't work.'*

Bobbajee – from the Hindi for chef, बावर्ची, pronounced bavarchi. This was used to refer to Army cooks.

Bobbery – another word that made its way from India with the British soldiers. This meant an argument, and became more widely known during the First World War.

Bobbing on it – waiting for something unpleasant to happen. It's easy to imagine inexperienced soldiers pacing up and down and fidgeting when they were waiting to go out on their first raid.

Bone orchard – a cemetery. This is yet another example of the trivialisation of death.

Booka – another word from the Hindi, भूखा, with the same pronunciation. It meant hungry.

Box-on – an Australianism, meaning a fight. Presumably this came from the sport of boxing. It could also be an order to stop fighting, although I haven't come across the origin of this meaning.

Box open, box shut – this is only referenced in Partridge and Brophy, but is supposed to refer to the practice of distributing cigarettes to those around you. The offer was only open for a short while, as cigarettes were scarce in the trenches.

Brass hats – a high-ranking officer. The name came from the golden embroidery on their caps. This is an example of the breach between the ordinary soldier and his superiors, and was meant to be derisive. '*We had communication trenches by which "brass hats" could visit us in the day-time.*'

Brasso king – Digger slang for an officer who orders that his men polish the brass on their uniforms, to keep them shiny.

Breadwinner – the term used by Australian soldiers to refer to their rifles. Many of the troops sent money back home. Australian privates earnt 6 shillings per day, British infantrymen were paid 1*s* 6*d* per day, and the Canadians received $1.10 per day (the ten cents was for overseas service).

Brolly – a facetious nickname for a parachute, the term came from regular civilian slang for an umbrella.

Bucked – excited. Interestingly, this meaning runs counter to the definition of 'buck', which was to refuse or resist, often with connotations of insolence. *'I'm bucked about the German withdrawal.'*

Buckshee – meaning free, there are some who say that the word came from Persian and others claim it originated in the Arabic. It was sometimes used to refer to what was left over. *'Is there any buckshee tea?'*

Bulls*%t – seemed to have various meanings among the troops: insincerity, Army disorganisation, or pretentiousness. There is discussion as to its origin, with some attributing it to the Australians, and others claiming it was an American word.

Bully beef – corned beef, a staple ration in the trenches. It is thought that the 'bully' came from the French *bouilli*, meaning boiled, but Doyle and Walker suggested that it could have been a reference to the pictures of bulls on the tin. It was often served in a stew, but could be fried. Once the soldiers got bored of eating it, it was given a new nickname, corned willie. This was a reference to the Kaiser, which goes some way towards explaining the general feeling about it. *'A frugal meal of bully beef, hard biscuits, and milkless tea.'*

Bumbrusher – an officer's servant, the implication being that orderlies were taken advantage of. This is another example of the contempt shown towards those of a superior rank.

Bumf – a contraction of bum fodder, which initially meant toilet paper. During the war it came to be associated with any kind of communication sent by headquarters.

Bund – bank or dam in Flemish, used by British soldiers.

Bunk in with – a Canadian expression, meaning to share a bedroom with. This is another example of a phrase that has remained in the language.

Buzz – this meant a signal sent by the telegraph operators, but soon came to be associated with rumours, as a quick succession of buzzes meant that there was news.

Byng Boys – the collective noun for the Canadians. It came from Lord Byng, the Canadian commander in 1917.

C3 – the worst possible health ranking. It meant that the man could not be sent on active service abroad. It became a reference to anything bad. '*My father was a C3 man.*'

Cagnat – a word adopted by the Canadians from the French, it meant trench in Poilu (French soldier) slang, but the Byng Boys used it to refer to barracks.

Camel – a type of single-seater scouting plane, built by Sopwith. It gained this nickname because of the hump above its machine guns. J. M. McCleery's diaries, edited by Guy Warner, show that many pilots died flying them. *'Brierley practically killed by spinning a Camel into the ground.'*

Camouflaged Aussie – an Australian term for an Englishman who was serving with the ANZAC soldiers. The term camouflage was, in itself, a new entry into the English language.

Canada – an alternative for No Man's Land.

Candlestick – a word for bayonet, describing one of its many uses within the trenches.

Canuck – what the Canadians called themselves. Indeed, they still do; one of the teams in the NHL is called the Vancouver Canucks.

Char – from the Hindi चाय, pronounced chai, which meant tea.

Charlie Chaplin's Army Corps – Canadian Casualty Army Corps.

Chat bags – underpants. Chats meant lice in the trenches, and they were everywhere – in clothes, on your skin, in your hair – so they understandably feature heavily in trench slang.

Chatting – another word based on the use of 'chat' to mean a louse. The hours of picking lice off each other were spent in small talk, so chat transferred to its modern-day use.

Chinny – another word from Hindi. चीनी meant sugar, and was adopted by the British forces.

Christen the squirt – to use a new bayonet for the first time to kill a man. This is rather a grizzly term, and highlights how desensitised to violence most of the troops had become.

Chubarrow – from the Hindi चुप रहो, pronounced chuparaho. This is another word picked up by British forces who had come into contact with Indian soldiers, and means shut up. It was sometimes abbreviated to chub.

Chuck it up – to surrender. From throwing your hands in the air.

Chum – formerly slang for an accomplice, this became a common word for friend in the trenches. Thieves' slang played a surprisingly important part in shaping trench language.

Civvy kip – the chance to sleep in a room with a bed: quite a treat for soldiers who were used to sleeping on 'biscuits'.

Clay kickers – shovels attached to men's feet to help them 'dig in'. This was a Canadian expression.

Client for Rouen – a man with venereal disease. There were over 400,000 cases of venereal disease during the First World War, which is perhaps unsurprising given that there were government-sanctioned brothels in the towns surrounding the Western Front. There was a specialist military hospital at Rouen that dealt with patients suffering from the disease.

Coal-box – heavy shell. There were several such nicknames on both sides of the trenches. This perhaps referred to the black smoke emitted when the shell exploded.

Cobber – a friend. This was mostly used by Australians, but was superseded by digger later in the war.

Cold footer – a man who is afraid of enlisting in the forces. Similar to the modern-day 'to get cold feet'.

Comforts Fund – shells. The Comforts Fund was set up in Australia at the beginning of the war to give help to soldiers. This was a facetious reference to that organisation.

Concrete macaroon – army biscuit. Another Australianism, referring to how hard the biscuits were.

Conk out – this referred to an engine failure. Later, it made the transition into civilian slang, and took on the additional meaning to die.

Contour chasing – flying at low level. This was also referred to as hedge hopping.

Cook's tours – a visit to the front by important civilians, such as MPs and journalists. This was usually only when fighting had died down for a while.

Cootie – a louse. I was surprised to learn that this word came from Cockney slang, as it is commonly associated it with American playground English.

Cop it/one/a packet – to die, or to be mortally wounded. Cop comes from the Old French *caper*, meaning 'to catch'. Packet probably referred to the shell the soldier had been hit by. *'She would get nothing ... unless I was to cop a packet.'*

Corpse factory – the false belief that German soldiers' bodies were sent back to their homeland to be burnt in factories. It was thought that they were melting the bodies to obtain fats.

Corpse ticket – a colloquial reference to an identity badge. As the war wore on there must have been, among many, the feeling that death was just around the corner.

Cow – an expression used mainly by the Canadians, but with some similar references in American English. It meant milk.

Crool the pitch – Digger slang meaning to ruin the chance of something.

Crummy – infested by lice and thus itchy; sometimes it was spelt crumby.

Crump – a noun and verb form of 'shell'.

Cubby hole – a small dugout. This was a very British term.

Cushy – from खुशी, pronounced cush, which meant pleasure in Hindi. It came to mean comfortable and often safe.

Cuthbert – a term used by all of the English-speaking forces, it started life in London then spread to general use. It referred contemptuously either to a conscientious objector, or to a man who was on administrative duties.

Dead soldier – an empty beer bottle. This is another example of the black humour that was everywhere in the trenches.

Dekko – from the Hindi देखो, which was the imperative form of 'to look'.

Delouse – a simple enough term, meaning to rid of lice.

Derby Men – Lord Derby was in charge of a scheme encouraging men to volunteer; it caused an upsurge in enlistment, but soon afterwards conscription was introduced.

Dhobi – another word taken directly from the Hindi. धोबी meant a laundryman.

Dhoolie wallah – wallah just meant a man, and was attached to almost any phrase. Dhoolie came from the Hindi for a litter, डोली.

Diamond dinks – 2nd New Zealand Rifle Brigade, from the shape of their shoulder patches.

Dick Shot Off – the ordinary soldiers' nickname for the DSO, which was an officers-only medal.

Digger – the most commonly used ANZAC term for friend.

Dingbat – an Australianism meaning a batman (an officer's servant). It was also used to refer to someone who was not behaving or speaking rationally.

Dinkum – Australian term meaning good. It could precede almost any noun. The 2nd Brigade, who fought briefly at Gallipoli, were known as The Dinkums.

Dixie – surprisingly, not an American term. In fact it was a mess tin used for cooking, and its origins are in the Hindi word देगची (pronounced day-gachy), meaning kettle.

Dodging the column – this term supposedly originated in South Africa, and was used in the sense of shirking unpleasant duties.

Dog – an Australian term meaning a swank, someone who was ostentatious and showy.

Domino – to kill. It has been suggested that this could come from an earlier use of the word domino to mean that everything was over, perhaps from the idea of dominoes falling over.

Doolally – insane. The word came over with the British forces in India, and was the name of a lunatic asylum in Calcutta.

Dope – had several meanings during the war. It could mean an absent-minded person, information or poison.

Driver's pint – a gallon. Drivers drank a lot, because their job was difficult.

Drop-short – any artillery that didn't quite reach its destination. When it was aimed at you, it was a blessing.

Drum fire – one of many musical terms to describe warfare. This described artillery fire, which sounded like a drum roll.

Duckboard – planks in the trenches to make it easier to walk on mud.

Dud – initially meant a shell that did not explode, but came to mean a failure in a more general sense after the war.

Dug-out – could mean a shelter under the trenches or a name for an ex-soldier who returned to serve his country; often these older men were less efficient than the younger soldiers.

Dum Dum – a bullet that expanded on impact.

Egg bomb – a small hand grenade. It got the name because it was roughly the size of an egg, and egg later took on the meaning of a bomb.

Emma Gee – Signalese for machine gun.

Ersatz – in German, this merely meant replacement. In an English-speaking context, it was used by both the Americans and the Brits to mean an inferior substitute.

Exasperator – slang for a respirator. It may have been cumbersome to wear, but it was vital in this era of gas warfare.

Eye-wash – seems to have applied to several situations on the front line. Fastidious preparation for an inspection by the officer was an eye-wash, as were idle threats that could not be carried out.

Fanti – came from the Hindi and was used to mean mad.

Fatigues – chores endured by front-line soldiers. They were necessary to keep the trenches working, but were not at all loved by the men.

Firing line – a simple enough phrase to understand, although worth including, as it has made its way back into modern-day English in a figurative sense.

Five-nine – also known as the 5.9, this was a high-explosive shell that caused much damage.

Fleabag – a British term for sleeping bag. It didn't matter where you went in the trenches, there would be lice.

Flybog – an Australianism for jam. Given that many Australian soldiers served in Africa, it is understandable that they would make this association, as flies would be attracted to anything sweet.

Flying arsehole – the badge for the observer corps in the RAF. It was an 'O' for observer with wings.

Foot-slogger – an infantryman. There were several other terms, both in English and in other languages, and most implied the difficulties encountered when marching.

Four-letter man – a s*%t, in the sense of an annoying man. There is an odd mixture of graphic and veiled language in trench slang.

Fresh faces in Hell – used in the expression 'there will be fresh faces in Hell', often uttered after an attack on the Germans. I have only found this expression in Australian English.

Funky villas – an amusing Anglicisation of Foncquevillers. Given that most British soldiers had only learnt rudimentary French at best, it is safe to assume that they had some difficulty with French pronunciation. Other examples include Eat Apples (Étaples) and Ocean Villas (Auchonvillers). See also Wipers.

Furphies – an Australian word for rumours. Often such rumours were spread behind carts, so as not to be seen by an officer; as the carts were made by Furphy, the word transferred use.

Gaff – temporary theatres built behind the lines. The lack of entertainment was one of the most difficult situations for the troops, and there are several references in diaries and letters to the need for music to raise morale.

Gasper – a cigarette. This term was used mostly by officers, in contrast with fag, which was an ordinary Tommy term. It had been in use before the war, but gained prominence.

Get the wind up – to be scared. The phrase was adapted, so that a soldier could be described as windy.

Give your arse a chance – an Australian expression spoken to people who wouldn't stop talking, it meant be quiet. The implication could be that the soldier was 'talking out of their arse', or that there would be consequences if they didn't stop.

Go binting – a term used when officers travelled into Cairo to visit brothels. It comes from the Arabic تنب, meaning girl.

Go crook – this meant to get angry and was used by Australian troops. Moore adds that it could also be used to mean 'to report sick'.

Go easy! – typically used by British troops when they thought that something was unfair or too much.

Go up the line – move from base into the trenches. There must often have been the sense that the front line was a conveyor belt bringing in replacement soldiers.

Go west – die. There have been several debates as to the origin of the phrase. Some say that it comes from the setting sun, others suggest that it could simply mean being transported back home (although this seems unlikely, as soldiers tended to be buried in cemeteries on or near the front line).

Gone dis – gone disconnected, of a signaller. This was worrying for everyone: it meant messages, potentially of an urgent nature, would not get through to the front line, and suggested that the signaller may have got himself into trouble, or even been killed.

Gone phutt – finished. The phrase comes from Hindi.

Gong – used facetiously to describe medals. Much of the trench slang suggests that medals were not always felt by the soldiers to be important. Perhaps they thought that it was inadequate recompense for what they saw and experienced on a daily basis.

Goodnight kiss – the last shot by a sniper at the end of an attack.

Goolies – name for testicles still in use today. It was brought back from India by the British forces stationed there, and comes from the Hindi गोली, meaning pellet.

Gorgeous wrecks – this was used to refer to a civilian defence corps made up of overage men, much like the Home Guard in the Second World War. The name came from their badge, which had GR on it. This stood for Georgius Rex, and was corrupted into gorgeous wrecks.

Grunt crusher – name for a tank. Grunt was a common term for an infantryman at the time, and crusher came from the fact that tanks could knock you down in your tracks.

Gup – this meant news or rumours (the two were very much interchangeable on the front line), and came from the Hindi गप्प. It was sometimes referred to as guff.

Guts – the heart of the matter. It had been used to mean courage since the nineteenth century at least, but presumably as a result of the common sight of guts on the front line, took on this new meaning during the First World War,.

Gutzer – a more graphic word for an 'abdominal', this meant a crash. During the First World War, it was used on a figurative level to mean 'failure'. The Australian National Dictionary website suggests that it could come from swimming, and the feeling you have after a belly-flop.

Have a field day – in regular Army usage this meant a practical training operation. To have a field day on the front line meant that everything had gone to plan.

Have by the short hairs – to have an advantage over someone. This is supposed by Brophy and Partridge to refer to the hairs on the back of the neck – it is painful when they are plucked. More recently, the phrase 'to have by the short and curlies' (meaning pubic hair) has been coined, but there is no evidence that the First World War equivalent referred to this part of the anatomy.

Have the breeze vertical – to be terrified. This derives from the use of 'wind' to mean fear.

Heinie – a Canadian expression used to refer to German soldiers. It came from Heinrich, a popular German name, and was also used extensively by the Americans.

Hobnail express – march. This came from the hobnail boots worn by the troops.

Hookem – a rule or regulation. The term comes from Hindi.

Hooza-me-kloo – a thingummyjig. There are several words for this in the trenches, but hooza-me-kloo was the preferred Canadian variant. This relates back to the difficulty in finding words for all the new experiences and encounters.

Hop it – die. It has been suggested that this phrase came from hopping over the top – soldiers were aware that the likelihood of surviving attacks and raids was relatively small.

Hot cross bun – an ambulance. This term came from the red cross on the side of these vehicles, and is another example of the attempt to detract from death, and render it less scary.

Housewife – this seems to have had two meanings. In the British Army it meant a sewing kit, but in the Canadian forces it was used to refer to the right arm, i.e. the one used for masturbating.

How many times? – a question asked of a soldier on retuning to the trenches after getting married. Soldiers' minds tended to revolve around certain things, and sex was high on the agenda.

Hughesilier – this is the name given to men in Australia who were given training as part of home defence. It is named after the Australian prime minister who fought for the conscription referendum.

Hump It – an Australian term used to refer to marching with your kit bag. Another comparison between soldiers and animals.

Hun – slang term for a German. This was widely used, particularly on the home front, and was one of many words used to mean the same.

Hung up on the barbed wire – dead. Often, soldiers struggled to get past the barbed wire when attacking, and stopping still to release yourself made you an easy target.

Iodine king – another name for a doctor. This came from the liberal use of iodine on the front line. King was a word frequently added in trench slang.

Iron rations – the basic Army rations, not at all loved by the troops. Sometimes this was also used to refer to shells.

Jake – colloquialism for 'good'. This term was used mostly by the Canadian and Australian troops.

Jam on it – luxurious. This was often spoken sarcastically, in a similar vein to 'you don't ask for much, do you?' Jam, in trench slang, appears constantly, and was clearly seen as the height of luxury.

Jerks – physical training. The phrase 'put a jerk into it' meant get a move on.

Jerry – yet another word used to mean German. This simply came from the beginning of the word 'German'. 'Jerry up' was commonly heard in the trenches when the Germans were flying overhead.

Jildi – meaning to hurry, from the Hindi जल्दी, pronounced jaldi.

Jock – the name for a soldier in a Scottish regiment.

Joy-ride – a leisure trip, not specifically in a car. It could be by plane, car or horse.

Joy-stick – used by the forces to refer to the controls of an aeroplane. Many of the pilots got a buzz from flying in dangerous situations and the exhilaration of travelling at speed. It was also a colloquial term for penis.

Kangaroo feathers – this amusing Australian expression means something impossible; after all, kangaroos can't grow feathers! It was also used to refer to the feathers worn by the Australian Light Horse.

Kapai – from the Maori for good, *pai*. This was a term used exclusively by the New Zealand troops.

Kicked in – killed, one of the many references to death developed by the troops in the war.

Kiltie – another word for Scottish troops, specifically Highlanders. Brophy and Partridge note that this was only used jokingly, and imply that it was not very popular among the Scots.

Kip-shop – brothel. The word shop was used quite generically to refer to any building. Kip could mean either a basic bed or to sleep.

Kitchener's Armies – Lord Kitchener made an appeal in 1914 for volunteers. Those who responded were referred to as Kitchener's

Armies and made up the numbers at the Battle of the Somme. It took them a long time to complete the necessary training, and when they got to the front they found that the regular soldiers resented them. Sometimes these men were also referred to as the Kitchener Mob.

Kiwi – worth including because it doesn't refer to what one would expect. It meant ground staff in the air forces, and came from the flightless birds. New Zealanders were referred to either in the generic ANZAC terminology, or as fernleaves from their emblem.

Knock off – this term had two meanings in the trenches: stolen (which has developed into the modern-day 'knock-off', meaning a fake) and to stop working, most commonly used in the phrase knocking-off time.

Kommando – originally used in South Africa, this word became common in the British Army.

It is still in use with its original meaning: a soldier who is trained to raid.

Lady Werfer – a Canadian phrase which refers to the German trench mortar. The troops picked up on the German use of the word *Minenwerfer* (mine thrower), and began to refer to trench mortars as Minnie and Lady Werfer.

Land crabs – a British expression meaning tanks, probably from the way they moved over terrain.

Larrigan – a Canadian waterproof boot. They were made of leather and were issued to Canadian troops in 1915.

Latrine rumour – a snippet of 'news' that was dubious, similar to gup. The term developed because Tommies would often sit in the toilets as a way of escaping the higher-ranking soldiers. They sat there reading newspapers and gossiping.

Lead-swinger – someone who shirks duties. This wasn't a particularly harsh expression, and would not be used to describe someone who endangered other soldiers. The phrase came from sailors – a sailor would be given the task of checking the depth as a ship came inshore, but would instead swing the lead plummet around and give false answers.

Leapfrogging – a practice whereby one group of soldiers would attack a trench, then hold it while another group attacked the next trench, then held it, so that the first group could attack the next trench, and so on.

Loos wallah – another use of the word 'wallah' simply to mean man. Loos came from the Hindi for thief, and loos wallah was used in this sense, as well as with the more general meaning of rascal.

Loot – from the Hindi for steal. Was also used to refer to a lieutenant, despite the British pronunciation of the word as 'leftenant'.

Louse trap – a sheepskin jacket that formed part of the soldier's winter uniform. It's easy to imagine why lice might like it...

Lousy – infested with lice. This was an unpleasant situation, which explains the evolution of the word into its modern-day meaning.

Lucifer – a match. The name of a popular brand.

Macaroni – the name given to Italian soldiers.

Mad minute – used as a reference to the British retreat from Mons, during which they were forced to fire very rapidly. In training, soldiers had to be able to hit a 4-foot target fifteen times in one minute from 300 yards away. One Scottish drill sergeant hit a 1-foot target thirty-eight times in one minute from 300 metres away.

Mafeesh : UK and ANZAC slang for 'nothing'. It came from the Arabic.

Maidan – a parade ground or space. The word was brought from India by the British forces stationed there.

Malum – to understand. This word also came from Hindi.

Massey-Harris – Canadian slang for cheese. Brophy and Partridge explain that it came from 'self-binder', which is a machine that cuts and binds corn in one operation. This seems rather a convoluted phrase, but gives us an idea of the backgrounds most of these men came from.

Methusiliers – this was a term used in the Australian forces to refer to a man who was over the usual age for combatants in active service. It is a combination of Methuselah (who is the oldest man mentioned in the Bible, said to have lived to the age of 969) and fusilier.

Mons man – a man who had served at Mons, and by extension had been in the original cohort of British Expeditionary Force soldiers in France.

Morning hate – a bombardment that regularly happened at the same time each day. The phrase came from the title of a popular song written by Ernst Lissauer at the beginning of the war 'Hassgesang gegen England' (hate song against England). The last three lines of the first verse were as follows:

> Wir haben alle nur einen Haß,
> Wir lieben vereint, wir hassen vereint,
> Wir alle haben nur einen Feind:
> ENGLAND!
> (We all have just one hate/We love together, we hate together/We all have just one enemy: England!)

Muck about – to wander aimlessly. This phrase was actually used by Kipling earlier than the war but was adopted by the British

Expeditionary Force. It probably took on a new meaning in the trenches, where everyone was surrounded by mud.

Muck in – a system whereby the Tommies organised themselves into groups and delegated tasks around. They would cook together, sharing food among themselves, and stayed in the same sleeping quarters.

Mufti – this was a word used by officers to denote civilian clothes. It came from the Arabic for free.

Mulligan – Canadian slang for a stew. This was in use before the war, but became more widespread during and after it.

Mush – guard room or cells. The *Oxford Dictionary of Modern Slang* does not give an origin for the word, but notes that it was mentioned in the *Athenaeum* in 1919, and suggests that it fell out of use during the First World War.

Mutt and Jeff – the British War Medal and the Victory Medal. The name came from two characters from an American cartoon of the time. 'Mutt and Jeff' began in 1907, being published in the *San Francisco Chronicle*, and went on until 1983.

Napoo – another corruption of the French, this word came from *il n'y en a plus*, there is no more of it. It quickly spread among the troops and became a universal slang word.

Nark – the origins of this word are said to be in the Romany for nose, *nak*, which in turn derived from the Hindi नाक. Its original use pre-war was in relation to informers (presumably because they stuck their nose into people's business, or sniffed out trouble), but this evolved during the war to mean a soldier trying to improve his standing by revealing other privates' secrets.

Nat Goulds – an Australian term meaning reinforcements. This was a sophisticated form of slang, derived from *Landed at Last*, the title of one of Nat Gould's novels.

Nip – an Australian and New Zealand term, meaning to borrow money.

O'Grady – the First World War equivalent of Simon in the game Simon Says. This was sometimes played as part of PT (physical training). Although we now consider this to be a children's game, an integral part of soldiers' training is to follow commands in a split second, so it would take a certain amount of strength to think about what had actually been said.

Old Contemptibles – a nickname for the original members of the British Expeditionary Force. They got the name from a reference by the Kaiser to 'the contemptible little' British Army.

Old soldier – an expression referring to Regular Army men who attempted to shirk duties.

There was certainly a divide between these soldiers and the new recruits who signed up to help with the war effort, and rookies were warned not to 'come the old soldier', meaning to pretend to know as much as, or more than, the old hands.

One over the eight – this meant 'drunk'. An average soldier was expected to be able to handle eight pints without being the worse for wear. It is worth noting that beer was less alcoholic in those days.

Oojiboo – another word meaning 'thingymajiggy'.

Open go – an Australianism, meaning that nothing was in the way of the person being referred to. Similar but different was 'a fair go', which meant you had the chance to do something, but there was the possibility that it might not work out.

Order of Bowler Hat – this was an officers' expression, and referred to men who were decommissioned and sent back home.

Oscar – an Australian term, meaning money. It came from the rhyming slang Oscar Asche (an actor), cash. It is interesting that it was not only the cockneys who developed rhyming slang.

Outfit – a unit or regiment. The word meant a group of travellers in the 1800s, and transferred to this military use during the First World War, probably as a result of the amount of marching soldiers did. The word was Canadian in origin, but spread through all the English-speaking troops.

Over the top – when soldiers jumped out of the trench and ran to attack the enemy. Many were killed as soon as they got over the parapet. This is probably the best-known word in trench slang from the First World

War. Also referred to as over the lid/plonk/bags.

Pahny – another word from the Hindi for water, पानी. This was certainly the time that Indian culture had most influence over the British language, and Hindi terminology was becoming accessible to a wider variety of people.

Pakaru – a term used only in the New Zealand troops, it meant damaged and came from the Maori.

PBI – Poor Bloody Infantry. There was a similar expression in French: everyone knew that the men at the front were having a miserable time in horrendous conditions.

Pear drops – a name for tear gas, because of its smell. Gas warfare was a very major part of the First World War, and this conflict saw the first use of tear gas.

Penguin – a similar word to kiwi, it referred to a member of the WRAF. They were not allowed to fly planes despite their involvement in the war effort. The Russian army was the only one of the major powers that allowed women to participate in active service.

Perisher – a periscope used in the trenches. Perhaps this came from the danger inherent in sticking anything over the top. Although it prevented the need for sticking your head over, there was still the possibility that you would be spotted and shot at.

Pip Emma – Signalese for p.m.

Pip, Squeak and Wilfred – British nicknames for the 1914 Star or 1914–15 Star, British War Medal and Victory Medal. They got this name from a popular cartoon strip of the era; the cartoon was printed in the *Daily Mirror* until 1956.

Point blank – wine, a corruption of *vin blanc*, with a subtle reference to the effect it could have on those who drank too much of it!

Pongo – an infantryman. There have been debates as to the origin of the word – some have suggested, it comes from 'pong', a colloquial term for a bad smell; others have make a link with Pongo, the dog from the popular Punch and Judy shows, who wore a hat similar to the soldiers'.

Poodlefaker – a man who was a bit too interested in his appearance and in seducing women; a dandy. Presumably this is a reference to the highly preened dog.

Pork and beans/pork and cheese – Portuguese soldiers. The reference was made because of the similarity in sound of Portuguese to these two expressions. Pork and beans was a staple Army ration, but never contained enough pork.

Posh – looking good. Partridge suggests that it came from a contraction of polish, and the term was also used to refer to a dandy, and in the verb form 'to posh up', meaning to smarten your appearance. It is commonly said that it is an acronym of 'port out starboard home' (the best cabins were on the port side when travelling from Britain to India, and on the starboard side on the return journey). However, many etymologists consider this to be a misconception, and Merriam Webster strongly refute the claim.

Potato mashers – a German grenade that looked like a potato masher. The handle made it easier to throw the grenade further.

Pozzy – ration issue jam. The term is thought to have its origins in one of the South African languages, as pozzy had meant a preserve there before the war.

Propaganda – officer slang for a rumour. This gives a flavour for the general feeling in the trenches at the time that nothing could be believed, as censorship was strict.

Puggled – eccentric or drunk.

Pukka – from the Hindi for ripe, पकाया, pronounced pakaya. It was used to mean real or authentic, and developed from this into its modern-day use as good or amazing, as evidenced by Jamie Oliver.

Pull-through – this was the name given to the long, thin cord used for cleaning a rifle. In slang, however, it referred to a tall, slender man.

Pung – Signalese for a nap while on duty at the telephone.

Pushing up daisies – dead. Similar phrases date back to the mid-nineteenth century, but this one was used more extensively during and after the First World War.

Put the fangs in – to request a loan. According to the Australian National Dictionary, there are examples of a similar phrase, 'to bite', with the same meaning from 1912.

Puttee – a cloth band wrapped around the leg to help a soldier walk. The word comes from the Hindi पट्टी, pronounced patti, which means a bandage. This word very much became a part of the English language, and was even used in the book *Cider with Rosie*, by Laurie Lee.

Rainbow – a term for a reinforcement who joined after the Armistice. The Australian National Dictionary Centre suggests that this may come from the imagery of a rainbow after a storm.

Rat and fowl – the slang term for the Australian shilling, supposedly from the depiction on it of a kangaroo and an emu.

Razzle – usually used in the sentence 'to go on the razzle', this didn't necessarily mean to get drunk, but it was heavily associated with going out and having a good time.

Red lamp – a brothel open to everyone (unlike the blue lamp, which was only accessible for officers). They could be recognised by the red lamps that hung outside them, hence the name.

Red tabs – an officer. They got this nickname from the red tab worn on their collars. They were sometimes known collectively as the red badge of funk.

Refilling point – the name given to the local dump (not in the sense of a rubbish tip, but a place where new weapons and ammunition could be picked up). As most soldiers visited the, they tended to be a place where rumours began and were spread.

Regimental – short for regimental sergeant-major, the senior warrant officer. It was often used as an adjective, and meant strict.

Roar-up – to abuse someone. This was an Australian phrase, and presumably came from the shouting.

RAMC – Rob All My Comrades. An amusing version of the acronym, which actually meant Royal Army Medical Corps. It was supposedly common for a wounded man's belongings to disappear while he was being treated or transported.

Rooty – from the Hindi रोटी, pronounced roti, which means bread. This is another word that was picked up the soldiers who served in India, and was brought back home, before being spread more widely in the trenches. There was also the term rooty medal, which was given for long service, the implication being that soldiers were given a medal for sitting around eating rations.

Rosella – a Digger term for a staff officer. A rosella was a brightly coloured parrot native to Australia, and staff officers wore gold and red, so the comparison was made and the name stuck, lasting into the Second World War.

Roughey – something hard to believe. The word is of Australian origin.

Rum jar – tightly packed drums of explosives that the Germans catapulted into the Allied lines. They got this name from their shape.

Rumbled – to be found out. This was used before the war, but became more widespread after it. It might have originated in the rumble made as rumours passed around and eventually reached the authorities.

Rush – swindle, or force to overpay. It was commonly used in the question 'how much did they rush you?'

San fairy ann – another bastardisation of the French, *ça ne fait rien* (it doesn't matter). This was used by all the English-speaking troops, who were willing to mock their own ineptitude.

Sausage – artillery shell or observation balloon. As we have seen, it was very common for weapons to be referred to using vocabulary related to food; perhaps this was because they were the two main aspects of war.

Schlenter – a South African phrase meaning fake, or not genuine.

Scrounge – to steal. Quite often things 'went missing' in the trenches, as getting hold of replacement items was difficult, or costly in the case of uniform. The word is supposed to have come from Northern dialect.

Send her down, Davy/Steve – let it rain! If you had to be on parade, it was better for it to rain, because it would usually be cancelled. Sometimes it was used in a more sarcastic tone.

Sergeant Major's – better than usual. Again, the division between the ordinary Tommy and his superiors was made clear through language: it was commonly felt that sergeant majors got the best items and passed the rest on to the men.

S*%t hot – enthusiastic. The word was actually used in a negative sense, when referring to a rookie soldier for example, and is generally considered to be a Canadian expression.

Short arm inspection/parade – medical examination of a soldier's penis to look for cases of VD. From Brophy and Partridge's description it seems to have been a particularly unpleasant experience, as men were lined up at random in a hut, rather than being seen individually.

Show – battle. Language related to the theatre was common in the war. The term was also used in the expression 'to put up a good show', meaning to perform well in battle.

Shrapnel – refers to paper money, apparently because it disintegrated quickly in wartime conditions.

Side kick – a Canadian term for a friend.

Silent death – this was a Canadian method of attacking the enemy. The Canucks would wait in no man's land until a German patrol came along; then they would ambush and stab them as quickly as possible to prevent the Jerries from making too much noise.

Six by four – the dimensions of toilet paper, and thus related to the slang term bumf.

Skittled – killed. This probably relates to the fact that men were knocked down like skittles as soon as they went over the top. This is an example of neutral language being used, so that death didn't have to be discussed openly.

Snuff it – die. This was probably a metaphor – extinguishing life just like a candle.

Soft job/number – a job that is easier than working on the trenches, even if it's boring.

Sore finger – someone who is overdressed. An Australian phrase potentially related to 'stick out like a sore finger'.

Souvenir – this term replaced keepsake. With people moving around more than they had in the past, and encountering new languages and cultures, it was inevitable that some foreign words would usurp the English ones. The word was also used to refer to a wound or to things taken from the battlefield.

Spit and polish parade – an inspection by the general of a group of soldiers.

Squad, halt! – salt. This was an example of rhyming slang in a military context – much of the terminology, including orders and weaponry, was new, so afforded novel opportunities for inventing rhyming slang.

Squarehead – British slang used to refer to a German. They were given this name because of the shape of their helmets.

SRD – painted on the rum jars (for Service Ration Depot) was known among the troops as 'seldom reaches destination'. It could also mean 'soon runs dry'.

Stand at ease – Army rhyming slang for cheese. It seems to have been a reasonably common form of forming slang words.

Steel jug – a helmet. The helmet was designed by Alfred Bates, and was sometimes referred to as a tin hat.

Stinker – a coat made of goatskin. Not only did these kinds of garments attract lice, they smelt foul, particularly when wet.

Stop a packet – also referred to as 'stop one', this term meant to be hit by a bullet.

Stoush merchant – someone who liked to fight. A 'stoush' was Australian slang for a fight.

Strafe – this was a German word adopted in earnest by the English-speaking troops. In German, its meaning is 'to punish', and it took on this sense (but was also used in noun form), as well as meaning a bombardment. Within the Australian army, it seems to have taken on even more meanings; according to the Australian National Dictionary Centre, you 'strafed a candle' (extinguish a candle) or were told to 'strafe it' (shut up).

Stray – a reference to bullets in the air. Naturally, there was always the possibility that you would be hit by a bullet.

Stunned – in Australian slang, this meant drunk. It presumably refers to the fact that you don't think clearly when drunk.

Suicide club – this was a term that referred to any group of soldiers that was being given a particularly difficult or dangerous mission. Traditionally, it was associated with bombing squadrons, but it could refer to others, including machine gunners.

Sweating on – excited about something (this was the opposite of 'bobbing on'). One assumes that this came from the concern that your request, promotion, etc., may not be agreed to.

Swinging the lead – the act of being a lead-swinger, as described earlier in this section.

Swipe – this was primarily Canadian slang, meaning to steal, perhaps because of the speed with which you would perform the action! It has passed into civilian speak seamlessly on this side of the Atlantic. Some dictionaries suggest that the word originated in American prison slang in the late nineteenth century, and that it potentially referred to a sweeping motion.

Take! – this was another Canadian expression, meaning good. Brody and Partridge mention that the British soldiers used 'take eight!', so perhaps these expressions were taken from card games, which were very popular on the front line. Crown & Anchor and House were particularly well loved.

Take the stripe – stripes in the Army denoted rank, so to take the stripe meant to accept a promotion. Moore comments that some soldiers chose not to accept their promotion as they preferred to stay with their pals in the trenches.

Tamasha – this is another word that came from the Hindi, तमाशा, which means a show.

The sheer number of borrowings from Hindi is proof of the amount of cultural interchange between Britain and India in the years leading up to the war.

Tannergram – the name for a telegram. Tanner in the trenches meant sixpence, which was the cost of a telegram from the trenches.

Tassie – an Australian and New Zealand expression, used to refer to someone from Tasmania.

Tear off a lump – the Australian National Dictionary Centre lists this as meaning 'to accomplish'. It appears to only have been used by the Australian troops, and is thought to come from the phrase 'to tear off a bit/piece', which meant to have sex.

Tear up for arse paper – to tell off. This was a phrase used mostly by New Zealand soldiers, but does seem to have made its way into the

British vocabulary at the time. It probably corresponds with the modern-day expression 'to rip to shreds'.

Temporary gentleman – this was rather a snobbish journalistic term for a man without any military experience back in Blighty who was promoted to the rank of officer on the front line. These commissions were only valid until the end of the war.

The good oil – this was an Australianism, and a step on from 'oil', which meant information. So, with 'good' in front, it meant true information.

The last hope – a facetious reference to standard Army rations. After several months of the same food, it's understandable that the men would be loath to eat any more of it, so they got what they could from an *estaminet*, a local bar-restaurant, or from those back home. If they were really hungry, and had no other choice, they would resort to their 'iron rations'.

The red badge of funk – used in a similar way to 'red tabs' to describe officers, because of the red marks they wore to distinguish them from other soldiers. On the front line, such colours were not allowed, as it made it easier for the Germans to spot individuals, so this use of colour on officers' uniforms, innocent though it seems, genuinely marked a difference, and went some way towards furthering the divide.

Thingumyjig – still used today, it initially seems odd that the term would have been invented in the First World War, but actually there were so many new gadgets, that it would have been difficult to describe or remember the names of many of them.

Third man – a superstition. The third man to light a cigarette was supposed to be unlucky, and thus would be shot. This is probably because the lighter would have to be on for a while in order to light three cigarettes, and so would be a good target. It is explained that anyone attempting to be 'the third man' would be swatted out of the way, so strong was the belief that it would result in tragedy.

Throw/chuck a seven – this was another Australian term, and meant to die. It is said to come from dicing. The Australian National Dictionary Centre also lists 'throw a six and a half', which means to almost die.

Tin hat – a helmet. The soldiers in trenches were not shy about showing their contempt for their equipment and uniform. That said, helmets came in useful on the front line, and were used for a variety of tasks: a basin for washing or cooking in, for example. A tin opener was another name for a bayonet.

To be winick – to be mad. Much like 'to be doolally', this phrase came from the name of a town where there was a lunatic asylum. In this case, it was the Winwick asylum in Lancashire (although Winwick is now part of Cheshire).

It was a Victorian hospital, built in 1894, and was standing until 1997.

To behave like a dog with two dicks – to be excessively pleased with yourself, and thus gloat, for example if you heard that you were being granted leave. This would be incredibly annoying in the confined surroundings of the trench.

To edge – an Australianism meaning to stop. The word supposedly comes from the use of edge to mean the limit. Once you get to the limit, you stop.

To get away with it – to escape unscathed from committing a military crime.

To give the wire – to warn someone subtly. This presumably came from the fact that barbed wire was not easy to spot when attacking the trenches at the other side.

To hump – an Australianism used to mean 'to carry'. Presumably, this comes from the fact that camels are used to carry things.

To zero – this means to study a rifle in minute detail.

Tourists – this was a term applied to the initial group of volunteers from Australia. Some thought that these young men were hoping not to be forced to fight, and thought they would just be able to use the experience to see the world while being paid. They were sometimes called six bob a day tourists.

Towelled up – an Australian term meaning someone had been punished harshly. It is claimed that the phrase 'oaken towel', from which this expression derives, went back to the eighteenth century.

Toy shop – where discarded weapons and equipment were kept. This is an extension of the use of 'toys' to mean weapons. The Americans referred to the war as a game.

Travelling Circus – this was the term applied to von Richthofen's squadron. The Red Baron, as he was known, shot down more enemy planes than any other fighter. It also referred to the practice of moving a machine gun squad from trench to trench, barraging the Germans as they went. Although it kept the Germans on their toes, it also meant retaliation.

Treacle miner – an Australian expression for a man who is constantly talking about his success back home.

Trench coat – this is still the term used to describe the long jacket worn by those in the trenches, and originated in the war.

Trench crawl – explains the slow pace on the way to the trenches. This was partly because of the obstacles in the way – such as shells, barbed wire or unlevel ground – and partly because the thought of going to the trenches wasn't one that was relished by the men at the front.

Trench foot – many of the men suffered from this ailment. The trenches were often very wet and muddy, and standing in water for a prolonged period of time led to swollen feet. There was even the possibility of frostbite in the long winter months. The soldiers would rub whale oil on their feet to help. Whale oil was also used as fuel for lamps.

Trez beans – the deliberate mispronunciation of the French *très bien*, meaning very good. Sometimes it was written 'tray beans' instead.

Typewriter – a machine gun, so called because of the sound it made. This is similar in nature to the French use of *moulin à café* (a coffee grinder).

Up in Annie's room – this term was used in response to a question about where someone was. It meant that you didn't know where the person was, initially with the implication that they were up to no good with a woman somewhere, but during the First World War it took on a new, darker meaning. If a man was lost, that was a serious concern, and probably meant that he had been killed.

Up to putty – what an Australian would say to mean useless. It derives from the pliability and softness of putty, and is similar in meaning to 'not up to much' in English.

Ventilated – an example of the dark humour that pervaded the trenches. This was a way of referring to a soldier's uniform after a battle, from all the bullet holes.

Vesta – a reasonably high-brow reference to a match. The term referenced the Vestal Virgins, who kept Vesta's lamp burning permanently.

Vigilance – the name for a rapidly put-together periscope used in the trenches. It was made by attaching a mirror to a stick.

Wad – a cake or bun. These were sold in canteens where you couldn't get alcohol, and Brophy and Partridge note the phrase wad-scoffer, meaning someone who doesn't drink.

Washed out – by the end of the war, a 'wash out' meant a failure in general, but its use began with the men who were rejected when trying to become officers: they were sent back to the regiments they had come from. It supposedly came from the practice of whitewashing over the marks left by bullets during target practice.

Well oiled – very drunk. The term oiled to mean drunk had been in use in the army for some time, but the mixing of normal men with seasoned soldiers spread its usage beyond the confines of the military.

Whack out/round – this meant to share out. Dish out was also used.

Whizzbang – the onomatopoeic name for a shell. It would hum as it flew through the air, then its flight culminated in a bang. They were very fast, so often weren't heard until they had already arrived.

Who called the cook a bastard? – a humorous and rhetorical question, meaning that the food was so bad that someone must have annoyed the chef. From the letters and diaries, it's easy to imagine this question being asked frequently, particularly as the soldiers got more and more fed-up with the same old food and stop-start lifestyle in the trenches.

Win – eighteenth-century thieves' slang for 'steal'. Thieves slang spread very rapidly in the trenches.

Wind-jammer – this phrase was used to refer to an officer who was known to refuse leave.

It eventually broadened in its usage to mean simply an officer who was not well loved.

Wipers – the comedic nickname for Ypres, because of the English-speaking soldiers' difficulty pronouncing its name. One of the popular trench newspapers of the day was named *The Wipers Times*.

Wooden overcoat – a coffin. A good example of the dark humour of the trenches.

Woolly bear – an artillery shell, which gave off lots of black smoke when it exploded.

Work a passage – to plan a scheme to get you back to Australia. Some soldiers pretended they had gone mad; this was referred to as working a ticket.

Wristwatch – amazing. This usage derives from the fact that a wristwatch was a luxury item. It seems odd today that a wristwatch would ever have been this exciting, but it was a rare sight in those days.

Yank – British slang for an American. There were several other terms, including Sammy and Doughboy. Yank was preferred by the Brits, particularly civilians.

Yellow girl – a woman who works in a munitions factory. Working with the chemicals used in munitions could turn the skin yellow.

Zeppelin in a cloud – sausage and mash. There are frequent references to zeppelins being called sausages, and this is another slang word that relates food and warfare.

Zero hour – the moment when an attack was scheduled to begin. This term derived from the counting down of the seconds to zero.

Ziff – an Australian term, of unknown origin, meaning a beard.

Doughboy

This section focuses on the slang used by soldiers from America and other member nations of the Entente Powers. The number of countries, and therefore the number of languages, involved was vast, and so overcoming the language barrier to find some of the lesser known foreign words is the most challenging.

It has been possible to find isolated examples of Greek, Russian and Italian slang from the period, but I am sure that there are plenty of examples that I have been unable to uncover.

The majority of the entries included here are French or American, whose slang is among the best documented; in general English-speaking nations have attached great significance to the study of colloquial language. The reason for the wealth of French material could be that nation's concern about the degradation of language (concerns were also expressed in American newspapers about the effects on English as a result of the First World War).

The French were involved in the war from the beginning, and so their slang had plenty of time to develop. Hence, we see several examples of slang words falling out of fashion (perhaps once their meaning was made clear to civilians, thus ruining the mystery surrounding them), and being replaced with new ones. France mobilised over 8 million troops from all over the country, and as a result the inclusion of diverse regional dialects in Poilu (the French nickname for a soldier) slang is one of its most distinctive features. The French also suffered a casualty rate of almost 73 per cent, so death and weaponry are frequently alluded to in their trench language. Another noticeable aspect of their slang is the tendency to combine words. Although the French language has two genders, and thus two forms of the definite article, they have not been included. In most cases, the literal meaning is given straight afterwards, followed by its actual use in the context of the trenches.

Although the United States only joined the war in April 1917, they used a wide variety of slang terms, possibly as a result of the number of English-speaking soldiers already on the front line. They certainly adopted some existing slang, and various humorous interpretations and mispronunciations of the French are evident in diaries and letters, as was the case with the British troops.

Doughboy was a name given to American soldiers. The word had existed since the seventeenth century, and initially referred to a dumpling or cake that was issued as standard rations. It took on the meaning of infantryman in the mid-nineteenth century, after the Mexican War. However, it was during the First

World War that the phrase became widespread. There are several theories about its origins – some say it was a reference to the buttons worn by infantrymen; others relate it to clay, which ran when subjected to rain and thus looked like raw dough. Others claim it comes from a corruption of the word *adobe*, which is a clay that gives off a lot of white dust. Americans were also known as Yanks or Sammies during the war.

~

À la noix – nutty. This actually meant unlikely, and probably derived from the fact that it was very difficult to get nuts on the front line. A variant was *à la noix de coco*, coconutty.

Abatage – to fell, cut down. Sharp reprimand.

ABC Powers – Argentina, Brazil and Chile.

Abeilles – bees. Shells.

Accroche-coeur – heart hook. Medal.

Ace – pilot who has brought down five or more enemy aircraft. Although this term and the one below were used by all English-speaking troops, particularly the Brits, it was very common among American troops. It came from the French word, *as*, which was used with the meaning of champion.

Ace of aces – a pilot who has brought down twenty-five or more enemy aircraft. Manfred von Richthofen, also known as the Red Baron, shot down a staggering eighty.

Acheter – to buy. In the trenches, this meant to mock someone, although it's difficult to know why. Perhaps it comes from the practice of paying for a slave or to sleep with a prostitute, and implies lack of respect.

Acting Jack – a temporary sergeant.

Aggie – an adjutant general, from the initial letters.

Ah-ah treatment – inspection of a sore throat, from the 'say ahhh'.

Aller au jus – go to the juice. Among the *poilus*, this meant 'to die', and came from the French use of *jus* to mean coffee, and one of their names for machine guns, *moulin à café* (coffee grinder).

Allo – the exclamation when a U-boat had been spotted.

Ammunition – pies and pastry, made by the Salvation Army and distributed in the trenches. It is extremely common in trench slang to refer to food as weaponry and vice versa.

Amocher – to make ugly. To wound.

AMT landing – a bad landing, meaning you had to be picked up by an ambulance, motorcycle or truck.

Anti-dérapant – anti-drifter. Wine.

Arbalète – crossbow. Gun. It was common to refer to modern weaponry using archaic terms.

Archie – anti-aircraft guns, also known as ack-acks. '*We didn't hear any bombs explode but Archie kept up a lot of fuss.*'

Arithmetic bug – louse. '*They added to our troubles, subtracted from our pleasures, divided our attention and multiplied like Hell.*'

Armoire à glace – mirrored wardrobe. Infantryman's bag. The bag shone when polished.

Army game – the way the Americans referred to the war.

Arrosage – watering (of plants). In practice, it was used with the meaning of 'bombardment'.

Another example of the trivialisation of horrific experiences.

Artiflot – a mixture of the words *artilleur* (artilleryman) and *fiflot* (the Parisian slang for artilleryman).

Asphyxier – to asphyxiate. To stun, in a more general sense. New words were being introduced during the First World War, and then were deliberately misused by the troops in their trench slang.

Asseoir – literally, to seat. The word was used to mean 'to stupefy', implying that the object is so shocked that they have to sit down.

Atterrir en pattes de mouche – to land with fly's feet. To land softly. This was an air forces expression.

Auber – this expression meant change (in terms of money), and came from the word *haubert*, meaning chainmail.

Auge – literally, trough. Soldiers often seemed to compare themselves to animals, perhaps they felt that they were seen by the authorities as such, so this was the commonly used word for a plate.

Aviator's lullaby – the sound made when a plane was shot by the enemy.

Avoir les foies – to have the livers. To be scared.

Avoir les grelots – to have the bells. To be shaking in your boots.

Babillarde – babbler. A letter.

Baby elephant – a corrugated iron shelter. Presumably it was so named because of the shape and colour.

Bafouille – mumbler. This was a similar word to *babillarde*, and meant a letter.

Bafouiller – to mumble. From the same root as the entry above, this word actually referred to an engine running badly, presumably from the low rumbling noise it might make.

Bagotter – to baggage handle. To march.

Baguette – once more, the use of food in military slang. This word referred to the military stripes worn on the leg.

Balancer – to balance. This meant to throw away, the idea being that soldiers were encumbered with so much kit that they couldn't stand up straight.

Baleinant – whaling/like a whale. Something that is so funny that it causes the listener to roll around like a whale.

Balloonatic – a balloonist. The term came from the combination of balloon and lunatic. *'Being a balloonatic must be terrifying.'*

Balochard – this was a term used to mean an idiot. It came from the word *baluchon*, meaning bundle, perhaps because those referred to didn't have things together.

Barbed wire garters/undershirt – this was a fictitious award, and was used when talking about someone who is clumsy or stupid. *'You've won the barbed wire garters for that manoeuvre!'*

Barbed wire disease – this was an American term for a breakdown experienced by those who had become prisoners of war.

Barchini saltatori – pole-vaulting ships. They were amphibious boats developed for use during the First World War. They were very slow in the water, and had to be carried aboard other vessels to the place they were attacking.

Barda/bardin – the French slang word for soldier's baggage. It came from a word used commonly in Algeria to mean the load a man or animal had to carry. These soldiers' bags were extremely heavy, around 70 lbs.

Barracks flying – over-exaggerating when talking about your flying prowess. Supposedly, it was often the non-fliers who were accused of this. *'Oh, Jones is barracks flying again.'*

Basket case – a man whose arms and legs have been blown off during fighting, and who therefore needs to be carried from the battlefield in a basket. Later, it's meaning was adapted, and took on a more metaphorical sense of helpless; now, we use the word mostly in the context of mental health.

Bath – used as an adjective to mean marvellous. This expression cam from Parisian slang, and relates to the city of Bath, which was widely regarded as elegant and beautiful.

Battle of Paris/Battle of Tours – the revelry that took place when the soldiers were back behind the lines and could enjoy themselves a bit. The author Jonathan Lighter gives this humorous example: *'I know some young chaps who have been more injured by ten days in Paris than by six months at the front. "The Battle of Paris" is the term we use here at the front.'*

Beak cover – the colloquial term for a gas mask. Beak had been used to mean nose for some time.

Becqueter – to pick up with the beak. To eat. In English, the word beak generally refers to the nose.

Belly-robber/belly-burglar – a cook. Army cooks were often suspected of keeping big portions of food for themselves. *'The belly robber had meat, and we just ate bully.'*

Benzine – to dismiss or remove an officer. The reference was to benzine's use for removing spots. '*He's been benzined.*'

Bite and hold – a form of warfare that involved constant attack, so that the enemy had to counter-attack. This meant that there was great loss of life.

Битье колесами сверху – the literal meaning is 'banging wheels on top' (pronounced bit'ye kolesami sverkhu). It was a method used by Russian pilots to break the fuselage of a plane – they would literally bang the wheels of their plane against the fuselage of the enemy aircraft.

Bobtailed – discharged dishonourably. It came from the verb to rob, which meant to remove, as the soldier's status was removed, and he was stripped of his stripes and papers.

Boche – German. It seems to have been in use since the mid-nineteenth century, but had a new lease of life during the First World War, and was adopted by many of the troops. In English, it was sometimes written bosche.

Boîte à asticots – a maggot box. The phrase refers to a gas mask, and comes from its shape and material, which made it look like a tackle box.

Boîte à poux – a louse box. This was a cap worn by the police. During the war, every soldier on the front line suffered from lice, and a cap would only serve to keep them in.

Bonbon – sweet. In reality, this was far from a pleasant thing; it was one of the names for a bomb.

Boot camp – a training camp, in much the same sense as it is used today. Boot was the word used to refer to a rookie soldier at this time.

Boulot – comes from the word *bouleau*, meaning birch. Birch is a notoriously difficult wood to work with, and so the word began to be associated with hard work, and is still used to mean job.

Bourrage de crâne – brainstuffing. Patriotic propagandistic newspaper articles. Many soldiers chose only to read trench newspapers, as those for civilians didn't accurately represent what they saw on a daily basis.

Bourrin – a dialect term from Anjou meaning a bad horse. It has roots in the word *bourrique*, meaning a donkey.

Bousiller – originally this term meant to do a job badly. Through the war it evolved to be used as 'to kill', as happened with so many other words at this time.

Bowleg – a cavalryman. The term originated from the fact that many mounted soldiers had bowlegs from riding so much. *'Hello, bowleg, come and give me a hand.'*

Boy scout – a name for an untrained soldier. Jonathan Lighter suggests that this could come from the hat worn by soldiers, but it's possible that it simply referred to the fact that the American troops were quite young (either literally or in terms of exposure to war).

Boyau – gut. In reality this meant a trench, and it was such a popular term that it passed into general use among the English-speaking soldiers too. They were probably referred to as guts because they zig-zagged, but it's possible that the word also made reference to the dirt they contained.

BP – an abbreviation for buck private. This was the lowest possible rank in the American army, and soldiers of this standing were viewed contemptuously.

Brains/brain squad – this was term used when referring to the intelligence officers.

Braise – 'embers'. This term was used by the poilus to mean 'change', in the monetary sense. 'Embers' was used in a metaphorical sense – 'il faut de la braise pour faire bouillir la marmite' (you need embers to make the cooking pot boil).

Bras cassés – broken arms. A lazy man.

Bucked – this meant proud or pleased, and didn't make it back into common usage back in America.

Bull ring – sometimes this referred to a training ring for horses, but more often than not it was used to refer to a training school for men who were going to the trenches. The term came from the ferocity of the trainers, and the harsh amount of exercise to be done.

Bunk fatigue – lying in bed, or sleeping. This term came from the use of fatigue to mean a chore. It was rare to get a chance to sleep on the front line, so advantage was taken whenever possible. *'He's probably doing bunk fatigue.'*

Bunk lizard – this was a negative reference to a man who got out of bed late, or spent all his time in bed. Presumably the name came from lizards' tendency to lazily bask in the sun.

Bunker plates – this was originally a term from the American navy. It was the name given to pancakes, and came from their shape, which was similar to the shape of coal chute lids.

Butcher shop – a hospital, or more specifically the operating theatre.

Ça murmure – it's murmuring. Used when a soldier felt like danger was on its way.

Cabot – dog. The name given to a French corporal.

Cafard – a cockroach. This meant depression, and was a common problem in the trenches. Many men had never left home before, and to be thrown into such a stressful and bewildering situation took its toll. Quite a few deserters gave this depression as a reason for disappearing from the trenches.

Cake walk – something that ends up being surprisingly easy. The term came from a dance in the southern states, traditionally performed by African-American slaves or minstrels.

Canard – duck. The name for trench newspapers and rumours. The word has made its way into the English language, meaning a lie.

Chandail – this is an example of two words being combined to make a new one. It is a body-warmer, and was invented in 1880 by a tailor from Amiens, but wasn't in general use until the war, when they were distributed to soldiers. Delvaux thinks its origins are in *marchand d'ail* (garlic seller), to whom the tailor originally sold the body-warmer.

Charrier – to transport, or move along. This was used to refer to a joke being taken too far. It is still used in the phrase *Il ne faut pas charrier* (often abbreviated to *faut pas charrier*), meaning 'you can't be serious' or 'don't get carried away'.

Châsses – the literal meaning was shrines, but it actually meant eyes. In an environment where your senses can literally be a matter of life and death, the eyes and ears took on a special importance.

Chauffer – to heat. This word had a dual meaning in the French trenches; it was either a synonym of 'to steal' or it was used to indicate that they were being shelled.

Chauve-souris – a bat (the French term literally means a bald mouse). This was used to refer to soldiers who flew at night; there were similar terms in German.

Чемоданов – literally meant suitcases, but was used to refer to shells (pronounced chemodanov).

Cheminée – chimney. This was another word used by the air forces. It meant to rise quickly in circles. Presumably the reference was to them looking like smoke from a chimney.

Cherrer – in the air forces, this verb meant to take the liberty of trying out difficult aerobatics. Among the soldiers at the front it was used to mean taking a joke too far. It probably comes from the French *charrier* (above). You could be a *cherreur*, or perform *cherrage*.

Cheval – a horse. It was quite common in the trenches to refer to an object by the way it was conveyed to you. On the front line, this word was used to mean a postal order.

Cheval de bois – a wooden horse. An aviation term referring to a mistake often made by rookie pilots: they would turn around on their wing when landing.

Chevron – military stripes in a V shape. The word passed into English, too. A chevron was added for each year of fighting the soldier had seen.

Chew someone's ass out/chew someone's balls off – to give someone a severe telling-off, presumably because of the ferocity of some of the officers. *'They're always chewing our balls off.'*

Chiasse – the noun form of the verb *chier*, meaning to s*%t. This was the colloquial reference to diarrhoea (the sh*%s).

Chiée – another noun form of *chier*. This meant a large quantity, so is the French version of 'a sh*%load'.

Chin chin – a term often heard in bars, it still endures today. It is said to come from the Chinese for thank you, 謝謝, pronounced cher cher.

Chiottes – yet another noun form of *chier*: swearing was inherent in all trench slang regardless of which army. This was the word used for toilet (the sh*%ter).

Chou – lettuce. In the trenches this was the term used for the head. It was also used in the expression *tomber dans les choux* (to fall in the lettuces), meaning to fall down after being injured.

Chtimi – someone from Pas-de-Calais, where there was an unusual accent. This name derives from their odd pronunciation of 'I', 'you' and 'me'. '*Voilà un chtimi.*'

Chuck a dummy – this meant to faint, or pretend to faint, while on parade. The impression given was usually that the soldier wanted to get out of doing any work.

Cibiche – the trench word for cigarette, presumably from the contraction of the words *cigarette* and *biche*, which meant darling, thus darling cigarette. Smoking was much more common during this period as a stress reliever, and a useful way of passing the time or bonding in the trenches.

Click for – this term meant to unexpectedly be given something. '*I have clicked for a position in the air force.*'

Click it – to be killed or injured. The expression probably came from the sound of a gun being cocked. '*A whole regiment clicked it today.*'

Cloud-creasing – artillery fire. '*We were cloud-creasing all day.*'

Cock and balls – one of the slang terms for an observation balloon. There was a similar

German expression; both come from the shape of the balloon.

Coffee cooler – a shirker. Presumably this came from the idea that they were waiting for their coffee to cool down before joining in with trench life. The phrase existed in the American army from the late nineteenth century, but gained in prominence during the war.

Collarbone camp – similar to the bull ring, this was the facetious name given to a training camp. Many of the soldiers injured their collarbones, or other parts of their body, during this training, which was harsh and relentless.

Colle – glue. This referred to rice, which was often overcooked in the trenches, and thus took on a sticky consistency.

Confetti – small-arms ammunition.

Cooler – a prison or cell. This was originally American thieves' slang, but passed through the troops on both sides of the Atlantic, and has endured. *'They threw him in the cooler for arguing with an officer.'*

Cossard – podded (of a pea). In the trenches, this was used to mean lazy. There is much debate about its origins: some claim it comes from the word *cossu* (well-to-do), with the implication that rich people are lazy; it could also derive from *cosson*, which is a type of beetle.

Cot jockey – someone who stays in bed as long as possible. There was a lot of resentment towards these men, as others were doing work or keeping busy in other ways while they slept.

Court-tout-seul – runs all alone. Cheese, presumably from the smell, which made other soldiers shun you.

Croix de chair – a fictitious medal for ground staff. The term was used in the air forces, and was a pun on the Croix de Guerre.

Croûte – crust/rind. This was a derogatory reference to food.

Cure-dents – toothpick. Bayonet

Danse – dance. It could refer to a windy day (this sense was primarily used in the air force), or battle. This is comparable to the English use of show to describe a raid.

Dazzle painting – this was a form of camouflage invented in the navy. It involved painting a ship in various bright, clashing colours. This made it difficult for the enemy to tell where the vessel was. It was used by both the British and American navies.

Death house – the name of the building where soldiers were trained in the art of gas warfare. *'Today was our first in the death house.'*

Débourrer – to unstuff. This verb was used in a similar way to 'do one's business'. Much of the slang used in the First World War was graphic in its imagery or nature.

Décollage – ungluing. This was used in the air force to refer to a take-off.

Déesse – goddess. The Direction des Étapes et Services (management of stages and services), which was in charge of the soldiers' health and supplies, among other things.

Dégommé – literally 'unstuck'. This was an adjective applied to an officer who was demoted, and the term made its way from French slang into English.

Dégonflé – deflated. This was a term used by the air force to mean depressed.

Dépoter son géranium – to take one's geranium out of the pot. In the trenches, this meant to be killed. It is a surprising reference given the atmosphere of masculinity on the front line.

Dock – this was sailor slang for a hospital. It played on the use of 'doc' to mean doctor and the fact that they would have had to dock in order to visit the hospital.

Dollar-a-year man – although it sounds similar to the Australian expression 'six-bob-a-day tourist', it actually had the opposite meaning; a dollar a year isn't very much! It was used to refer to a man who was serving because he wanted to represent and protect his country, rather than because he wanted the money.

Doublard – a doubler. This was a word used to refer to a sergeant major, and came from their two golden stipes.

Dovetail – a man who had graduated from officer training, and was waiting for a commission when the Armistice ended the war. There was a similar expression in the Australian forces – 'Noah's doves'.

DP – this stood for daisy pusher, so meant a dead man.

Dream sack – a navy term meaning a hammock, for obvious reasons.

Dry canteen – a canteen that didn't sell any alcoholic drinks.

Easterner – a man who thought the army's efforts should be focussed on the Eastern Front, and that this would swing the war in the Entente's favour.

Eau pour les yeux – water for the eyes. This expression was employed when referring to any alcohol, and plays on *eau-de-vie*, meaning brandy. It probably refers to the effect this alcohol would have on a soldier's ability to see straight.

Egg wagon – a plane used for bombing. Bombs were referred to as eggs, potentially because they were dropped out of planes from a height. *'Here comes an egg wagon.'*

Eighteen-pounder – *not* a cannon, as might be assumed. This was an affectionate term for a young recruit; these men probably could not have imagined what they would be met with when they got to the trenches. It was a problem; the armies were so desperate for troops that they stopped checking ages; Britain's youngest soldier was twelve, but several thousand underage boys signed up for Canada (the youngest was ten).

Empiler – to pile up. An expression used when a vendor charged extortionate prices, presumably because he was piling the cost on to the buyer.

En écraser – to destroy it. To sleep. Sleep was a very powerful coping mechanism, as soldiers could forget what had happened for a short while.

En jeter – to throw it. This meant to work hard and put effort into what you were trying to do. It sounds very similar to the English 'throw oneself into'.

En jouer un air – to play a song. In the trenches this meant to run away; *flûte* was a word for leg.

Entraver – this came from the French *entrevoir* (to glimpse), and meant to understand. It was an old Parisian slang word, but spread through the trenches.

Epilé – shaved. This was meant to be in direct contrast to the *poilu* (hairy). Having lots of hair was seen as a sign of virility and therefore courage, so those who shirked duty were referred to as without hair to highlight their cowardice.

Épingle à chapeau – meaning 'hatpin', this was one of the many terms used when referring to a bayonet, presumably because of its shape. At this time, women's hatpins were very long and sharp, much like a bayonet. *'Nous partons au combat l'épingle à chapeau au fusil'* (we're going into combat with hatpin guns).

Epluchure – peeling. This was the term used for a shell explosion. Perhaps it referred to the effect on the body if you were hit by one.

Escalier – staircase. This was an aeronautical expression meaning to descend in fits and starts, as though walking down a staircase.

Escarpins – high heels. This was an ironic reference to the army-issue boots.

Escoffier – a very old French word for a tanner, it came to be used with the meaning 'to kill' during the First World War.

Etat-mâchoire – a facetious pun on the word *état-major*, meaning headquarters, from the similar sound. *Mâchoire* means jawbone, so perhaps implies that they never stopped giving orders.

Être bon jusqu'au trognon – to be good to the core. This expression implied that someone was being exploited, but was such a good person that they allowed it to happen.

Fadé – meaning well off. It was used in an ironic sense on the battlefield, and originally came from thieves' slang (which also influenced English trench slang), where it meant to share the loot from a robbery. If a man was referred to as fadé in the trenches, the chances are that he was wounded, ill or in a dangerous situation.

Faire la tortue – to do the tortoise. A funny expression meaning to fast, because tortoises have curved backs; the implication is that if you start to get a rounded stomach, it's time to stop eating.

Faire le poireau – to do the leek. It meant to wait. Leeks take a long time to grow, and can spend a substantial amount of time in the ground without any damage being done to them, so this could be the source.

Fanal – beacon or lantern. This was slang for the stomach, perhaps because having a full belly made the situation seem less bleak. *Je n'ai rien dans le fanal* (I have nothing in my stomach).

Faucheur – reaper. A name given to a type of cannon.

Fer à repasser – a flatiron. This term referred to a plane that didn't glide.

Fighting on the cognac front – drunk. The term cocgnacked was also used.

Filon – vein (of minerals). This was used to mean a lucky man, probably because anyone who finds a vein of precious metal is very fortunate.

Flaming coffin/flaming hearse – this refers to aeroplanes, which could easily catch fire, as well as posing the obvious danger of crashing or being shot down.

Fokker fodder – anyone fighting against a Fokker in an inferior plane. The Fokker was an effective aeroplane for the Germans during the war.

Four-minute men – a derisive term applied to those on the home front in America, who would go to the cinema to watch the four-minute news reel, and ridicule the German propaganda.

FTD – feeding the dog. The phrase used to describe a soldier who is killing time. The similar expression in use in Newcastle, England, 'walking the dog', means going to the pub.

Fusains – spindles. Legs.

Gadget – this term began life in the navy, before passing into the army. It meant a mechanical instrument (so was used in a similar way as 'thingummyjig'). *'Pass me that gadget.'*

Gagner la croix de bois – to win the wooden cross. There was exactly the same expression in English. It was a facetious reference to the Iron Cross, with the meaning to die. If you were killed in the trenches, you would be buried with a wooden cross.

Galloping freckles – a name for lice. *'All I can think about is my galloping freckles.'*

Garde-mites – the louse guard. This was the man who was in charge of the clothes shop. Lice played a big part in life on the front, and they are one of the most commonly referred to phenomena in trench slang in all languages.

Gaux – this word comes from *sergot*, the town sergeant, and means lice. It is most likely a reference to how unwanted both were on the front line!

Gendarme – policeman. This was a nickname given to the Fokker planes, perhaps because they were so good at chasing down other aircraft.

Genoux creux – hollow knees. This term referred to a man who didn't do much. It was often used as an insult: '*Viens nous aider genoux creux!*' ('Come and help us, lazybones')

Gimper – this was American air force jargon for a friend you could rely on; it's understandable that this would be important to those fighting in the air together.

Ginglin – a reference to *Saint-Glinglin*, meaning Doomsday. This was used as a term for a shell explosion.

Gniaule/gnôle – a term from Auvergne, meaning brandy. With such mixing of men, it was inevitable that some regionalisms would make it in to the national language.

Gold brick – this seems to have had several uses among troops. It meant an inexperienced and incompetent army officer, but could also refer to someone who was trying to shirk his duties, a military policeman or an ugly girl. Jonathan Lighter gives an example of the second use in a letter: '*We were given twenty-four hours off duty, which started many a "Goldbricker's" career.*'

Goldfish – canned salmon. This was used fairly commonly in the trenches, and the men must have become sick of eating the same thing over and over. '*All we have to eat is goldfish.*'

Golf course – this was used to refer to any ground that had been heavily bombed or shelled. It acquired this name from the craters left.

Goopher – another American air force term. The hierarchy among the soldiers dictates that a goopher is just below a gimper in terms of ability. Dixon quotes Eddie Rickenbacker: *'When a new chap arrives, he's an egg. All good eggs soon become vultures, and they are promoted to goopher standing.'*

Go over the hill – yet another expression used for 'to die'. This presumably came from the action of going over the top of the trench, and the likelihood inherent in that of being killed. *'My friend went over the hill yesterday.'*

Grass-cutter – the name given to a training plane that couldn't be used for flying. Cadets spent around a month in these before getting to go up.

Gratte-ciel – scratch the sky/skyscraper. A tall man.

Grave – this referred to a cubby hole, or fox hole, in the trenches. This is another example of the soldiers' morbidity. After a while in the trenches, many must have wondered when their time would come, and expected it anytime.

Grifeton – this was another word for an infantryman, and comes from the slang *grive*, meaning both guard and war, so *griveton*, which became *grifeton*, means a guard and a fighter.

Groundhog Day – the American slang term for the day the Armistice was signed. Supposedly it got this name because the soldiers could finally come out of their holes in the ground, and referred to the tradition of marking the day as the first sign of spring.

H hour – the American term for zero hour.

Hand grenade – this is another example of the interchangeableness of words for describing weapons and those describing food. This actually meant a meatball in the American army, presumably because of the shape.

Hedgehop – flying low, with the implication that the pilot is so close to the ground that he has to move the plane up every time he comes across a hedge.

Hibou – an owl. This meant a pilot who flew during the night. A similar expression was in use in German.

Hitch – refers both to enlistment and to the period a soldier has enlisted for. It is thought that the term comes from the use of hitch to mean get married, thus implying that the soldier in question had married himself to the army. *'I'm going to take on another hitch.'*

Hosteau – this word was used to refer to a hospital, but intentionally rhymes with *château*. For soldiers during the First World War, a visit to the hospital was not the negative thing it seems to us today; it gave the opportunity for a break from the front line.

Hotel de Barbwire – an example of the Franglais that developed during the war. This term was used to refer to a prison. *'I'm off to the Hotel de Barbwire.'*

Hurleur – yeller. This was the name for an infantry observer. Without access to a telephone, they were forced to shout corrections that needed to be made.

Hurry up and wait – a mocking order often issued to American troops by their fellow soldiers. It highlights the suggestion from those above that men should always be doing something, and quickly, but that actually there was nothing to do in many cases.

Hyphenate – a name for an American soldier of foreign descent, from the label 'Italian-American', for example.

Installer – to install or establish. This was used by French soldiers when a man was showing off, and might just as easily refer to an individual as to the German forces during a bombardment.

Jack Johnson – a heavy German shell. The term supposedly came about as a reference to the boxer of the same name.

Jarretière – garter. This meant a group of musicians; they earnt this term because they carried their drums and bugles around their necks.

Jawbreaker – an army-issue biscuit, so called because they were so hard. This is also suggested by the Australian term 'concrete macaroon'.

J'en ai marre – this has remained in French language, and means 'I've had enough' or 'I'm bored of this'. It is thought to come from a very old French word, *marri*, which meant annoyed.

Jusqu'au boutiste – to the ender. A soldier determined to fight until the war is won.

Хорошо – the Russian word for 'good', pronounced khorosho. Many of the prisoners of war came back with a rudimentary knowledge of Russian.

Lame d'acier – strip of steel. A thin man.

Lampe – in French, it's literal meaning is lamp, although it is often used with the sense of 'quaffer'. It means mouth, and comes from the slang verb *lamper*, which existed pre-war and meant to knock back or quaff.

Lance-pierres – literally, this means a slingshot, but in the First World War it was applied to guns. This is similar to the use of 'crossbow', and is another way for the soldiers to mock the equipment they've been provided with.

Latrine telegraph – similar to phrase latrine rumour, this meant news that was spread about by word of mouth.

Lattes – slats. This was the word used for shoes in the trenches. Presumably this was because the standard army boots were so uncomfortable, and afforded little protection.

Légumes – vegetables. This actually referred to high-ranking members of the armed forces, so *les grosses légumes* (the fat vegetables) is the French equivalent of the English figurative use of the big cheese.

Lest – with a literal meaning of ballast, this word shows the strength of friendship and respect between comrades that developed during the war. In practice, it was used to mean an observer in a plane, and it implies the necessity of having such a man on board; their role was considered a very valuable one.

Liberty cabbage – the American term for sauerkraut. Anything German was prefixed with 'liberty' for some time.

Limace – in modern French, this word means slug. However, the word as used in the trenches bears no relation to this, and instead means a shirt. It comes from the Old French *lime*, which meant a file, because traditionally shirts and blouses were made of rough material.

Loin-du-ciel – far from the sky. This was applied in noun form to a very small man, and is a good example of the use of gentle mockery in the trenches to form bonds.

Loufoque – I have included this as an example of butchers' slang, which existed before the war but was brought to the attention of the masses during it. The rule was that you added an 'l' to the beginning of the word, send the first letter of the word to the end, and then added a suffix. So, *loufoque* actually meant *fou*, crazy or strange. Another variant of the same word was *louftingue*.

Louper – this means to fail, and is still commonly used today. It is thought to come from an old French word, *lope*, which refers to a piece of something that is hanging down loosely.

Machine à coudre – sewing machine. This was a nickname for a machine gun, from the sound it made.

Mail-order – this was a term for an incompetent new soldier who has recently arrived from training as an officer. This presumably refers to the fact that they were sent over when needed on the front line. *'Oh no, we've got another mail-order officer.'*

Maous – large. This was a regionalism, but spread in to general use as a result of the war. A home front territorial soldier was referred to as a *maous pépère* (a big granddad).

Marmite – literally means a cooking pot. In fact, it referred to a shell.

Marraine – godmother. It was common for women to look after the soldiers on the front, by taking them in for a few days or sending them some letters with extra provisions. These women were very well loved by the men in the trenches.

Marron – chestnut. This was one of the slang terms for a bullet, presumably from the shape. It was also used in the phrase *flanquer un marron à quelqu'un* ('to throw a chestnut at someone'), which meant to hit someone.

Marsouin – porpoise. This was a term used to refer to the Marines. It came from the movement of a porpoise in and out of the water, as Marines were in a similar situation – sometimes on land, sometimes in the sea.

Marteau – a hammer or drill. This meant crazy or mad, perhaps with a similar etymology to 'screwed' or 'nuts'. '*Il est marteau*' (he is mad).

Mettre en boîte – put in a box. This expression actually meant to make a mockery of someone.

Mettre les voiles – 'set the sails'. This was used to mean 'flee', as was *mettre les cannes*, 'put on the canes'.

Mittglommer/mittwobbler – this meant a 'handshaker', someone who was always trying to curry favour with his superiors.

Moulin à café – coffee grinder. This was another term used to refer to a machine gun, from the noise it made.

Mousetrap – the nickname given to the plant where Lewisite was produced, because employees were not allowed to leave until the end of the war, in order to prevent the secret of its manufacture from being circulated.

Musiciens – musicians. A name for beans, from the sound your stomach made once you ate them.

Musique – music. This actually referred to a bombardment, so is similar to the use of vocabulary from the stage in the English-speaking troops.

Mustard imitator – the colloquial term for Lewisite, a gas produced by the Americans. It was produced and used in retaliation against the mustard gas used by the Germans. It was said to be seventy-two times more deadly than any other gas used in the war.

News room/news office – a reference to the kitchen, which was just as influential in spreading rumours as the latrines! I suppose a lot of people of varying ranks would have spent time in the kitchen, getting food, so they cooks may have been privy to information not normally accessible to the troops.

Ничего – the Russian for nothing, pronounced nichego.

Нет добра – a Russian phrase meaning not good, pronounced niet dobra.

Night-bombing – this expression was used to refer to spending some time with a woman after dark. *'I've been up at the estaminet doing some night-bombing.'*

Ninety-day wonder – many officer training schools lasted for just ninety days, so a newly commissioned officer was referred to by this expression.

Nouba – this comes from the Arabic نوبة, which is the name for the music played at parties in Algeria. In French, it was used simply to mean party.

OD – stood for olive drab, the colour of American uniforms. It came to mean army issued. Lighter quotes a song of the time:

> My shoes are full of O.D. dirt,
> My hair of O.D. glue

This shows just how versatile a term it was.

Office – a term used in the airforce to refer to the cockpit; after all, they *did* do their work in the cockpit.

Order of the Shovel – a fictitious award, won by being killed in battle. The term suggests that what you are doing will lead to your grave being dug.

Ours – a bear (the animal). It was common in the trenches to refer to a horse as another animal, and normally these references were derogatory, as is the case here; an *ours* is an old horse.

P and P – this stood for piss and punk. Punk meant bread in American army slang, so this referred to a diet given to those being punished. It consisted simply of bread and water. *'We just sat and ate our P and P.'*

Panier – basket. This referred to the dock for observation balloons. It is interesting that a place where something, or someone, rested was called a basket – the same is true in *pagnoter*, which is related to *panier*.

PCDF – Pauvre Couillons du Front, poor dicks at the front. Everyone recognised that life on the front lines was a miserable existence.

Peau de toutou – lamb skin. This phrase was used in sentences such as *le faire à la peau de toutou*, which meant to tell an improbable story.

Pedzouille – a hayseed. This referred to a man from the country, and by extension to someone stupid or clumsy.

Péniche – barge. This was another name given to shoes. Perhaps it came from the situation a lot of men found themselves in of having the wrong sized clothes.

Perco – a shortened form of *percolateur* (percolator). This was a name given to a rumour, presumably because it percolated from the higher ranks through the trenches.

Physical torture – the military slang for PT, physical training.

Pick 'em up and put 'em down – one of the terms used for marching. *'It's time to pick 'em up and put 'em down.'*

Pistol Pete – this was the term used to refer to an officer who was overly strict and aggressive with his troops; it was usually a substitute officer.

Pognon – in the hand. Money.

Poilu – literally 'hairy'. This was the name by which French infantrymen referred to themselves. Being hairy was seen as a particularly virile trait, and thus represented courage. There is no evidence that this was used in a derogatory or self-deprecating way; in fact, it is still seen as a sign of masculinity in many cultures, for example in Turkey.

Popsqueak/pipsqueak – another onomatopoeic term for a German shell, from the noise they made when flying over, or into, the trenches. *'They're sending over a popsqueak.'*

Possum playing dead – a dud shell. This was slang used by southern American troops.

Poteau – literally pole or post. The word was used to mean friend, and this usage continues to the present day. It is supposed that the word developed its current meaning because you lean on your friends.

Пожалуйста – 'please' in Russian, pronounced pozhaluysta.

Prendre la pipe – to take the pipe. French expression, meaning to be beaten.

Prune picker – the nickname given to a Californian. This was a term used in the navy, and references the many orchards and vineyards in the state.

Punaise – insect. The word was used to refer to a loose woman, so was perhaps a shortened version of *punaise de lit* (bedbug).

Put wise – this was an Americanism that came to be adopted on both sides of the Atlantic. It meant to show a rookie officer over the trenches. Many of the men sent over, whether as officers or Doughboys, really had no idea what awaited them, and no amount of preparation would have been sufficient. The trench was therefore a place where you had to learn from experience, by doing.

Quart de brie – wedge of brie. Nose.

Quedalle – this comes from an old French slang word, for money, *dalle*. *Ne comprendre que dalle* (to only understand money) implies that you don't understand much, and this translated into use as nothing. *'Je vois quedalle'* (I see nothing).

Queue de rat – rat's tail. This was the name given to one of the German grenades with a particularly long pin, approximately 40 cm long. These grenades could be launched in a gun or by hand.

Rabiot – an example of a military word that existed before the war. In the trenches it was often referred to as *rab*, and it meant whatever was left. It could be used in the context of anything being distributed – food, money, tobacco, etc.

Raisiné – grape juice. Blood.

Rampant – creeping. This was an air force insult aimed at those who didn't fly planes.

Raquette – racket. This was the name for a hand grenade, presumably because the action of throwing a grenade was reminiscent of hitting a ball in tennis.

Rase-mottes – 'scrape the earth'. A term used by French aviators to describe flying very low.

Raseterre – scrape the ground. A short man.

Read one's shirt/the news – this was a facetious reference to checking one's shirt for lice. It happened with such regularity, and was done so attentively, that it came to be referred to in this way.

Reste-à-terre – stay-on-the-ground. A term used by the French air force to refer to those who didn't fly planes.

Ribouldingue – a mixture of the words *ribouler* and *dinguer* (both of which mean to roll in dialect). It meant joy or hilarity.

Ricochet officer – an officer who was sent to fill in in emergency situations. Presumably the name comes from the fact that they were being ricocheted all over the place covering for diffeent people.

Roule-par-terre – roll on the floor. Brandy, because of the effect it could have on soldiers.

Ruptured duck – a damaged plane. It was quite common to refer to aircraft as ducks.

Sachi – a mysterious French army word, whose origin has not been documented. It was used to mean things are going well in contrast to the word sachipa, which meant that things weren't so good. Presumably, *sachipa* was formed by adding *pas* (not) to *sachi*, and later the 's' from *pas* disappeared.

Sammy – this nickname was given to American soldiers by the French. It was an allusion to Uncle Sam.

Sardine – yet another food term used to refer to military concepts, in this case a non-commissioned officer's military stripes.

Sauce – literally, this means sauce. In the First World War, it was an air force term for petrol. '*Remets la sauce*' (put your foot down).

Scuttlebutt – a gossip. This seems to have been a navy term, and could also mean a rumour. Generally the rumours they told were viewed as unlikely. *'What's that scuttlebutt saying now?'*

S'envoyer – to send oneself. In the trenches it meant to eat. *'Je m'envoie du pain'* (I'm eating bread).

Se bilotter – to store up bile. This meant to worry, and was probably a reference to feeling sick when worrying too much about something. *Se faire de la bile* (literally, to do bile to oneself) is still in existence with the same meaning.

Se défiler – to unthread oneself. In practice it meant to run away or escape.

Se l'accrocher – to hold on to it. Oddly, this term was used to mean 'to do without it'. *'On s'accroche du vin'* (we do without wine).

Se mettre à genoux – to kneel down. This was an expression used in the air force to describe landing nose-first.

Se mettre la ceinture – to put on the belt. To choose not to eat.

Se pagnoter – to put yourself in a basket. This meant to go to bed, probably because the beds were uncomfortable.

Se tasser – to pack oneself. This came to mean 'to eat', because soldiers needed to be full, if possible. *'Je vais me tasser du pain'* (I'm going to eat some bread).

Sea gull – a navy airman, for obvious reasons.

Sea lawyer – a navy term used to refer to a seagoing soldier who is particularly argumentative.

Seam squirrel – another term for a louse; the words used became increasingly inventive as time went on, although this term is said to go back to the late nineteenth century. Lice were also referred to as pants rabbits.

Séchoir – clothes dryer. In the trenches, this meant barbed wire, as a rather grim reference to the possibility that you would be caught by it and left there to die.

Shellitis – the fear of warfare. When the horror of the conflict sank in, it could cause shock.

Ship over – to re-enlist. This came from the need to come back over by boat. *'I ship over next week.'*

Singe – monkey in French. This meant corned beef, and shows how the soldiers felt about their rations.

Skirt duty – looking for women to spend time with. *'I'm going on skirt duty.'*

Sleeping dictionary – a woman from the country the soldier is posted in and whom he is having sex with. The idea was that you could learn more of the language from her than you could any other way.

Slum – this was the name given to a beef stew. It had several names, depending on its consistency: slum with an overcoat (with a crust), slum with the tide in (watered down), and slum with the tide out (slightly thicker). *'Slum again this evening.'*

Snap out of it – to get out of bed. Its current usage – similar to 'wake up' or 'stop dreaming' in a more figurative sense – probably comes from this meaning.

Snow digger – the nickname given to a soldier from New England, where the average snowfall is between 35 and 100 inches per year, depending on where in the region you are.

Snowbird – the nickname given to a man who signed up at the beginning of winter so that he would be guaranteed a job, something to eat and a place to stay, but then deserted when the weather improved.

Sore-ass/sorerump – another phrase used to mean a cavalryman. Naturally, riding all the time would be uncomfortable. *'Are you going to be a sore-ass?'*

SOS – a pun on the proper use of SOS to mean save our souls: in the First World War trenches, this was used to mean same old slum.

Souffrante – 'suffering'. It meant 'match', and was a play on words on *soufre*, meaning 'sulphur'.

Спасибо – the Russian for thanks, pronounced spasibo.

Старый человек – 'old man' in Russian, used to refer to the commanding officer (pronounced starii chelovek).

Stonkered – has its origins in the Italian *stanco*, meaning tired. It came to be used by American and British troops during the war.

Submarine – this was a reference to the ability of submarines to submerge themselves and thus be unseen. It was used by American soldiers to refer to hiding in order to avoid doing work.

Tabac – tobacco in French. This was used when talking about gruelling fighting. It's interesting that the word would be used in this negative sense, as smoking was a part of the war on all sides of the trenches. Perhaps it referred more to the need for a cigarette after enduring such an experience.

Tartines – slices of bread. This was another use of food in slang, and meant shoes. The word was sometimes also used in the term *en faire un tartine* (to make a sandwich out of it), which meant to exaggerate when telling a story.

Tartre – the literal meaning is limescale or plaque. It was a term used by the air force to mean bad or unfavourable. '*C'est tartre, cet avion*' (this plane is bad).

Tâter – to feel. This was used in the expression *tâter le manche*, meaning to try to fly solo, and *savoir en tâter*, to know how to fly.

Taupe – a nickname for German soldiers, from the colour of their uniforms.

The jump-off – the American expression for going over the top. The place where an attack is launched is also referred to as the jumping-off point.

The tooter the sweeter – another example of the Franglais used in the trenches, this term meant the sooner the better. It probably came from the French phrase *tout de suite*, meaning straightaway, but could also come from the word for early, *tôt*.

Ticket west – a wound that is guaranteed to result in death. This expression presumably derived from the phrase 'to go west', meaning to die. *'He got a ticket west.'*

Το γερμανικό – pronounced 'toe yermaniko', this literally meant the German. It was used to refer to the hours between 2 a.m. and 4 a.m. when the Germans often raided, knowing that most of the troops would be asleep, or at best tired.

Tôle – sheet metal. Prison.

Tomber sur un os – stumble upon a bone. This expression was used to denote an unpleasant surprise. It's easy to understand why even the idioms used began to be based on morbid matters.

Toubib – meaning doctor, from the Arabic الطبيب.

Товарищ – comrade, used more colloquially as friend (pronounced tovarishch).

Trenchitis – a term used to explain the feeling of missing home and being fed-up with the situation. It also combined feelings of frustration and fear, and was referred to even by higher-ranking soldiers. *'The men are suffering from trenchitis.'*

Turn off the juice – turn off an engine. Juice meant petrol in general, but was used most commonly when referring to planes.

Un fort caillou – a real pebble. This was a reference to a bad, or stupid, soldier. Its use is similar to 'blockhead' in English.

Undercarriage – a term used by pilots to refer to legs.

Vache – cow. This could be used either as an adjective or as a noun, and was used to refer to superiors who were considered too harsh. The origin of the word in this sense is Parisian; before the war, in the capital it was applied to policemen.

Vaseline landing – a smooth landing.

Verni – the literal meaning is polished; however, in the context of the First World War, the word was used to mean lucky.

Vide-boche – an boche-emptier. This was a word for a bayonet, with the implication that it was used to empty Germans.

Vidé – empty. Used to mean 'tired'.

Vieille noix – old nut. A boring man.

Vitrier – glazier. This was used to refer to a footsoldier, because the bags they carried, when polished, reflected the light, like a window.

Waffle tail/waffle-seater – this was a nickname for staff officers, who used to sit in a slatted chair for so long during the day that their trousers looked like waffles.

Waltzing Matilda – an American name for Australian soldiers. It came from the song, which was written by an Australian of Scottish descent. The song was very popular during the war.

War baby – aside from the obvious meaning of a child born to a soldier during the war, this could also mean a young, inexperienced officer. It was used contemptuously, much like ninety-day wonders.

Webfoot – a nickname for an infantryman, presumably because of the difficulty of walking in the trenches, which were muddy and full of water. Brits still say that they expect to evolve webbed feet because of the amount of rain.

White mule – a strong whisky. It was made of corn, which meant that it was light in colour, and its taste was said to have a kick! It was also known as white lightning.

Wise-guy section – the Intelligence section. This was a play on the military terminology.

Woodbine – an American term for British soldiers, from the brand of cigarette popular among the Tommies.

Woolly bear – the effect when a shell burst. There was thick black smoke, and it moved around like an animal, hence the likening to a bear.

Я не понимаю – I don't understand, pronounced ya ne ponimayu.

Yellow cross – mustard gas. So named because the containers and shells for this gas in liquid form were marked with a yellow cross. '*They died, because they didn't notice the yellow cross.*'

Yellow ticket – a dishonourable discharge. It was so named because of the colour of the paper used to print it.

You'll find it on the payroll – an expression used when a soldier lost some of his kit in reference to the fact that, eventually, he would have the cost of it deducted from his pay. For this reason 'showdown inspections', during which officers would check soldiers' kit bags, were feared. *'We had a showdown, and anyone who was missing something, found it on the payroll.'*

Your number – this referred to the personal number carried by all American troops. If a bullet had your number on it, it meant that you would be hit by the bullet. Equally, if you lost your number, that meant you had been killed.

Zèbre – zebra, meaning a good horse. There are far more slang words relating to bad horses than to good, but nevertheless it is clear that they played an important part in life on the front.

Zigue – a way of referring to a friend. It comes from the word *gigue*, short for *gigolo*, but isn't a negative expression. '*C'est un bon zigue.*'

Zigouiller – a regional slang word for stab, it entered into general usage during the First World War.

Fritz

In total, the Central Powers mobilised almost 23 million soldiers during the war. All of the countries involved in this alliance were based in Europe, although the Ottoman Empire spread into Asia and Africa.

The use of slang in the German and Austrian forces has been very well documented in both German and French, and thus German makes up this section of the book. There is a great similarity between German and Entente slang – in some cases, exactly the same words or images are used. The majority of the slang that can be found relates to weapons and fellow soldiers.

It is surprising, but true, that there hasn't been much research into Slavic military slang, supposedly because it has tended not to be used in the written form. For readers with an interest in other Central Powers trench lingo, there seems to be some contemporary documentation of Hungarian slang, but unfortunately it has been difficult to access it.

It should be noted that German has three genders, but they are not included here. It is also the practice in the German language to capitalise nouns, but not verbs, etc., and I have capitalised this section in accordance with those rules. As with the previous section, a literal translation is given in most cases, then an explanation of the actual usage of the word.

'Fritz', the title of this section, of course applied to the Germans. It came from the diminutive form of Friedrich, and was one of the more polite ways of referring to the enemy. Other terms, such as Boche and Hun, were regularly used, too.

~

Abbauen – to disintegrate. This meant to fall behind on a march, and presumably comes from the implication that those who fell behind were either wounded or really struggling, emotionally or physically.

Abendsegen – the evening blessing. The word was used as a nickname for the evening cannonade. This is a similar expression to the English term 'morning hate'.

Abführen – to lead away. In practice this word meant 'to wound'.

Abgebrannt sein – to be burnt away. This meant 'to be penniless', and bears a striking resemblance to the English phrase 'money to burn'.

Abgekrepelt sein – to be dog-tired, from *krepeln*, meaning to advance with difficulty.

abgesägt werden – to be sawn. This phrase was used for a soldier who had to pay for the round.

Abonnent – subscriber. The nickname given to any plane that was regularly sighted over German lines.

Absatz – the heel. This was a nickname for an orderly, and could refer to the job – orderlies were at officers' beck and call, so they were always at their heels. Alternatively, it could mean that they kept everything running smoothly.

angstschiessen – to fear-shoot. It was said that the Entente troops shot at the Germans late at night because they were afraid of being attacked.

anhauchen – to breathe on someone, with a meaning of 'to annoy'.

auf Vordermann gehen – literally, 'to go on the man in front'. This was used to refer to a girl losing her virginity.

Badeurlaub – bathing holiday. This referred to the very rare occasions when a soldier would be able to sleep in a proper bedroom; after a long time in the trenches, this would seem like a real luxury.

Bajonettvergolder – bayonet gilder (in the sense of covering something with gold). The phrase was used to mean a man who is masturbating.

Benzinhusaren – petrol hussars. This was a nickname for members of the automobile corps.

Blauer Max – blue Max. A German medal, the Pour le Mérite (French was the Prussian court language at one time, and was spoken across Europe). It was associated with Max

Immelmann, a German fighter pilot, and was bright blue in colour.

Büchsenöffner – can opener. This was the German word for a bayonet. There were some very similar expressions in other languages.

Bummsköpfe – boom heads, a term for infantrymen. This represented the feeling that infantrymen were the most likely to be killed in battle.

Chausseekitzler – road tickler. This was the name given to those who worked on road- or railway-building duties.

Damen aus der Hölle – women from Hell. This phrase was associated with the Kilties, who went into battle wearing a kilt. The claim that they were also known as the devils in skirts has been proven false – in fact it was an American journalistic invention!

die Dachdecker arbeiten – the slaters are working. This expression was used when the machine guns were firing. Presumably, it relates to the noise.

die Läuse alarmieren – to alarm the lice (to scratch oneself).

Dreckfresser – mud glutton. This was the name by which the German infantrymen called themselves. The mud is a common theme in trench diaries and letters, and was by no means limited to the Germans.

drei Appels plus Weidenkorbflechten – three songs and wicker basketmaking. This was the nickname for a day off, because they tended not to be enjoyable.

du verdammtes Aas – you rotten carcass. This was a graphic expression, meaning 'you stink'.

durch die Scheisse gezogen werden – to be pulled through the shit. This meant to have the mickey taken out of you.

ein lackierter Affe – a painted/varnished monkey (a snob).

einen affen haben – to have a monkey. Used when a soldier had been drinking alcohol; supposedly this comes from the soldiers' behaviour when they'd had a few too many.

einschieben – to slide in, meaning to go to sleep.

Englands Schrecken – England's fear. The Germans' term for a zeppelin. The Brits had reason to be scared: over 500 people were killed by zeppelin raids during the First World War.

erst abwarten dann Tee trinken – first wait then drink tea. This is a surprisingly British-sounding idiom, meaning let's not get carried away.

Etappenhengst – stage stallion. This referred to someone who pretended to be very brave but slipped to the back of the line when it came to actual danger. It could also be used to refer to the officer in charge of each stage.

Falle – trap. Used to refer to a bed, perhaps because the temptation of sleep was always there. Soldiers from both sides of the trenches complained about the lack of sleep.

Fassade – façade, used to refer to the face.

Fässellesklopfer – a barrel beater. This was the German name for a machine gun, because the noise sounded like that made by a cooper when making barrels.

Festungsschwamm – a fort sponge. This was an Austrian term used as a nickname for men who put on weight because they were guarding small garrisons, and thus didn't have much to do.

Fettigkeiten – fatness. Anything fattening was probably a luxury in the trenches, and so any kind of luxury item began to be referred to in this way.

Franzmann kocht Kaffee – Frenchman is cooking coffee. Clearly the Germans knew of the French use of *moulin à café* to mean a machine gun, as this phrase meant that the French had started using their machine guns.

Frontschwein – front pig. A name for the troops at the front. This use of pig is similar to the English 'grunt', comparing the men in the trenches to animals. Many felt that their lives were considered irrelevant.

Fußlatscher – foot traipser. Another word used by the German infantrymen to describe their job. There are several similar French and English words that imply an equal distaste for the amount of marching to be done.

Galgenschieber – gallows profiteer. This was a nickname for the court martial auditor.

Garderobenständer – an ironic name for a man who is famished, and has thus lost weight.

Gardelitzen – literally, guard plaits, but actually it referred to the regiment-specific stripes worn by soldiers. The word was used as a nickname for noodles, because they resembled these military stripes.

Gefechtsziege – fighting goat. This was the nickname for a captain's horse. Such disparaging names were common throughout all the armies.

Hämorrhoidforscher – haemorrhoid researcher. This was a nickname for nurses. On the front line, the soldiers' complaints were often fairly ordinary, and could have been prevented in other circumstances.

Heidenangst – pagan fear. Usually this was used in the sentence *er hat eine Heidenangst* (he is scared stiff). This was a time when religion was very important in society, so it probably referred to the idea that those who were religious had no reason to fear death.

Heldenkeller – heroes' cellar. This simply meant a shelter. Perhaps it was an ironic reference to the fact that to stay alive and be a hero, you had to take cover.

Heldenseminar – heroes' lesson. The nickname for a training school. Everyone coming to the front hoped to come back home a hero.

herabtrudeln – to coast down. This was an aeronautical term used to describe a plane being shot repeatedly and thus crashing.

Heringsbändiger – a herring restrainer. This was the name given to army grocers, who were thought to keep the best goods for themselves.

ich denke der Affe laust mir – I think the monkey is delousing me. This expression meant I'm amazed; I imagine most of us would be amazed if a monkey started to delouse us.

im Wurstkessel sitzen – to sit in the sausage cauldron/pan. This meant to be in a difficult situation.

in den Aether hinaufzischen – to fizz into the ether. This was a term used by the air force to denote flying up through the air.

Insektentöter – insect killers. This referred to cigars sent by those on the home front, and probably referred to insects' tendency to fly towards the light, which in this case would kill them.

Intelligenzbörtel – this was an Austrian expression, and translates as an intelligence tube. It meant the yellow and black military stripes that represented a year's service. The implication was that you had to be intelligent to have lasted so long.

Invalide studieren – a rather pessimistic phrase, meaning to study an invalid. It referred to those people who were considered unfit for service, and could have implied that they were making a bigger deal out of their inability to fight than was necessary, because secretly they didn't want to fight.

Irrenanstalt – asylum. This was used in the sentence *du bist von Irrenanstalt entsprungen* (you've escaped from the asylum), meaning you're mad!

Janitscharenmusik – Turkish soldier music. This was a nickname for syphilis; it seems quite unusual, since the Turks were fighting *with* the Germans, not against them.

jemanden anpumpen – to tap someone. This meant to ask for money or to steal. It might imply the thieves' trick of banging into someone to steal something from them. It is similar to the English phrase, to tap someone up.

Jungfer – bull's eye. This is how the cavalry referred to their swords.

Jungholz – young wood. The nickname given to rookie soldiers.

Jux – joke. This was a Bavarian word, and meant an apple puree. It suggests that the German soldiers were less than happy with their food.

Kaffeesäcke – coffee bags. This was a term for trousers, because they were made of a coarse canvas fabric.

Kälberzähne – calves' teeth. This was a nickname given to the gruel served at officer training camps.

Kalbfell – calfskin. A nickname for a drum. A drummer was known as a *Kalbfellschläger*, meaning a calfskin hitter.

Kammerjäger – chamber hunter. A nickname for a non-commissioned officer responsible for uniform.

Kanalschiffe – canal boats. This was a nickname for the soldiers at Erlangen, and came from the canal there.

Kanarienvögel – a nickname for the men of the 118th regiment, because they had yellow shoulder straps.

Kaninchenlöcher – rabbit holes. This was the name given to 'cubby holes'; the trench systems were often complicated and wound in and out to reduce the damage if a shell hit, so they probably seemed like a warren.

Kanonenfutter – 'cannon fodder'. The Germans' use of this word to mean infantryman is quite well known, and tallies with the British impression that those above didn't care about the welfare of those on the front line.

Kapitulantenabzeichen – sign of surrender. This was the nickname for a pickaxe, presumably because if you resorted to the use of this as a weapon, you were in a bad situation.

Karboldragoner – carbolic dragoon. This referred to members of the medical corps, probably because of the widespread use of carbolic acid during the war.

Karbolkaserne – carbolic barracks. Following on from the theme in the entry above, this meant an ambulance or hospital.

Ladenbiene – shop bee. The name given to a shopgirl. *Biene* was commonly used when referring to women.

Lamontierbrett – whining board. This was the slang term for a violin, and must refer to the noise made by this instrument, particularly when played badly.

Landhase – land hare. This was the name for an infantryman, presumably because they moved in similar fits and starts over the ground.

Landwehronkel – a land army uncle. The name for an officer in the territorial army.

Lappen – rag. A nickname for someone who has been in active service for three years. At the end of such a long period of fighting, anyone would have looked tired.

Latsch – shuffle, slippers. This word referred to the foot.

Laubfrösche – leaf frogs. This was a nickname for soldiers, presumably because they hopped about through the foliage.

leichte Infanterie – light infantry. This was a nickname for lice, probably because it seemed as they were always marching over and attacking the soldiers.

Leuchtkäfer – a nickname given to those operating searchlights. It meant glowworm or firefly.

Maulschuster – a muzzle cobbler. This was the slang term for a dentist.

mit einer Affenfahrt steigen – to climb like a monkey. Often soldiers had to climb trees in order to get a better shot.

Mündung – spout. This is a rather unpleasant reference to the anus. The reality is that life in the trenches did not agree with many of the soldiers, so they often suffered from dysentery.

moralische Katzenjammer – an emotional hangover. The Germans used this phrase to describe depression, which was a serious problem in the war. Men who became depressed often did foolish things, or tried to get themselves injured in order to go home.

Müllergesell – a miller's assistant. This referred back to the French slang for a machine gun, *moulin à café*, and meant a man who had no back-up but was armed with a machine gun.

Müllschippen – rubbish shovellers. A slang term for hands.

Nachtenbummler – night loiterer. This was a reference to the lice, which seemed to trouble the soldiers more in the evening, probably because they had nothing to think about, but also potentially because the beds were full of lice.

Nachteulen – night owls. This was another name given to spotlight operators.

Nachtkübelschwenker – a chamber pot slinger. A rather unpleasant word for a nurse.

Nachtwandler – sleepwalker. This was a term used in the air force when referring to a reconnaissance plane that flew at night.

Neuschrapnell – the British were not the only soldiers who bastardised French place names; the Germans did the same. This means new shrapnel, but was the nickname for Neufchatel.

Oberverdachtschöpfer – senior suspicion-creator. This was the nickname given to the adviser to the war department.

Ohlala – the nickname for French soldiers among Germans.

Opiumfritz – opium Fritz. This is interesting, because it shows that the Germans also adopted the nickname Fritz in their slang. It referred to a non-commissioned medical officer, because of the practice of giving out opium to those who were injured.

Orgel – organ. This was actually a nickname for a cannon.

Plappertasche – blabber bag. This was the nickname for a cartridge belt, because the sound of guns firing was said to be like chattering.

pochen – to knock. In the German-speaking trenches, this meant 'to go on a march', presumably because of the noise made by the soldiers' boots.

Porzellankiste – a porcelain box. A nickname used by the air force to refer to an aeroplane that has already been damaged or has broken.

Potsdamer – a man from the Potsdam regiment. The Potsdam only accepted men of the highest physical caliber, so this term was used ironically to refer to a man who wasn't very fit.

Pulverbienen – powder bees. This was how men who worked with gunpowder were referred to. The implication was that their job was a hectc one.

qualmen – to smoulder. This took on the meaning to smoke, and is now commonly used in the expression *wie ein Schlot qualmen* (to smoke like a chimney).

Querbeet gehen – to go across the bed. This meant to go off on manoeuvres all over the battlefield.

Rachenpulver – revenge powder. A nickname for cheap alcohol or brandy.

Rattenkasten – rat cages. In the trenches, it was used to mean a vehicle used to transport troops.

Rauhbeine – raw legs. A nickname for new recruits. Anyone who had spent any time in the trenches grew used to the constant marching, but new recruits would have trouble adjusting.

Rennverein – running club. A sarcastic nickname for the Russians, this term is said to have come from the quick retreat made by Russian soldiers.

Rollschuhläufer – roller skater. A nickname given to shells, because the noise they made was similar to that made by a roller skate when it hit the floor.

Salonschuss – living-room shot. An injury that wasn't too serious, and thus meant that the soldier would be treated to a rest for a while.

Schenkwasser – gift-water. This meant alcohol, which was very highly prized among the soldiers.

schnell – quick, quickly. In the air force, speed was the most important thing, and so the meaning of the word broadened to mean good or beautiful.

Sterngucker – stargazer. This is another nickname for the soldiers who manned spotlights. They played an important role on the front line, because they allowed the anti-aircraft gunners to attack planes before they reached the trenches.

Stuttertante – spluttering aunt. Yet another nickname for a machine gun, again from the noise it made. Perhaps surprisingly, many of the weapons used were referred to as women.

Strohsackwalzer – straw-mattress waltz. This was the nickname for a retreat, presumably because there were so many straw mattresses around that you had to dance around them to get out of the trench and away to safety.

Suppenpott – soup pot. A facetious nickname for a helmet, although it's entirely possible that some soldiers did use their helmets as a bowl.

Taschenkrebse – pocket crayfish. This was a nickname for grenades, and came from their shape, which was like a lentil.

Teelöffel – teaspoon. The facetious nickname given to a shovel. It was common in all languages for the soldiers' equipment to be mocked. No one felt that they were adequately prepared for the situations they faced.

Tinte – ink. This was used in a number of contexts. A *Tintenlecker* (ink licker) was a man who worked in an office, and anyone *der Tinte gesoffen hatte* (who had guzzled ink) was mad.

Totenschein – death certificate. This was a nickname for an ID badge. We see similar references in both English and French.

trocken gesetzt sein – to be sitting dry. In soldier speak, this meant to be broke (in the sense of to have no money).

Trübsalspritzer – misery sharpener. In the trenches, it was almost unforgiveable to admit defeat or to be negative, so anyone who was a pessimist was given this nickname.

U Boot – an *Unterseeboot* (submarine). In fact, this was often used, rather graphically, to refer to bedpans in a hospital environment, or could mean a corrugated-metal shelter.

Überschwung – loosely translates as extra push. This was an Austrian term used to refer to a belt, presumably because it forced the soldier wearing it to stay fit, it being very tight, and to keep going.

umdrehen – to turn. In German soldier slang, this meant to stay out all night.

Unterstandsmarke – dugout brand. During the war, soldiers were often sent cigarettes and cigars with encouraging or patriotic messages; this was the nickname for them.

Urlaubsschuss – a holiday shot. In a similar way to the Entente troops, the German soldiers saw a minor injury as a good thing, as it gave them the chance to leave behind the trenches for a while, and be looked after in the hospital.

Vereinigungsknüppel – unification stick. This was the nickname given to the flag; perhaps it was facetious, or maybe it simply made reference to the fact that the German men were required to fight for their country.

Vereinsabzeichen – the club's badge. This referred to the Iron Cross; if you got one, everyone knew you had done something very brave, and so everyone wanted to know you and be friends with you.

Verschönerungsrat – the beautifying council. A nickname given to hairdressers or barbers.

Viehtrieb – cattle drive. This was the nickname for the marches young soldiers were forced to take part in, while being overseen. It is another example of soldiers feeling that they were treated like animals by those in authority.

Vizespieß – vice-skewer. One of the many nicknames given to vice-sergeants. There was also *Vizejesus* (vice Jesus).

Vogelfutter – bird feed. The Entente Powers' troops were not alone in their distaste for the food at the front. This referred to a kind of gruel made from millet.

Wagenschmiere – vehicle grease. This was a term used to mean marmalade, and is interesting in that the English-speaking forces used a similar term, 'axle grease'.

Wau-Wau – woof woof. This term could have two meanings. It was used to refer to an officer in the barracks, but could also be used as a nickname for the Entente Powers' anti-aircraft guns.

weisse Werke – white works. This was a term used when referring to operations or positions on the Eastern Front, where there were several chalky regions.

Wischer – a noter. This was a regionalism, and meant a prescription, but spread into general use during the war.

Wolkenkratzer – a skyscraper. This term took on the meaning of a plane during the war. For many soldiers, this would be the first time they had come into contact with the machines so closely.

Wulewuhs – a bastardisation of the French *voulez-vous* (do you want?). This term was used to refer to French soldiers.

Zahnstocher – tooth pick. This term was also used by the French military, although they used it to refer to a bayonet. Among the Austrian troops, it meant a spear, and in German aviation it referred to a dart or an arrow.

Zaster – dough, but used to mean pay or wages. It is interesting that the same use of dough is current in English-speaking countries.

Ziechhoch – it was not only the English-speaking troops who had difficulty with the French language. This is a bastardised version of the French word *seau* (bucket), which was pronounced *siau* in some of the regions of France where fighting occurred.

Ziehharmonika – accordion. This was the nickname given to the book of notes carried around by staff sergeants.

Zielerkränzchen – aim garland. This facetious nickname was given to anyone who did extra target practice. *Ziel* in German can mean an aim literally or figuratively.

Zweispeisefaster – two-meal faster. It was common in Austrian training camps to use starvation diets as a punishment, and this was the name for a trainee soldier who received this treatment.

Bibliography

Ayto, John and John Simpson, *Oxford Dictionary of Modern Slang* (Oxford University Press, 2010).

Bergmann, Karl, *Wie der Feldgraue Spricht* (Gieszen: Töpelmann, 1916).

Brophy, John and Eric Partridge, *The Long Trail: Soldiers' Songs and Slang 1914–18* (London: Sphere Books, 1969).

Cook, Tim, 'Fighting Words: Canadian Soldiers' Slang and Swearing in the Great War', *War in History*, 20(3), 323–44.

Déchelette, François, *L'Argot des Poilus* (Paris: Jouve & Cie, 1918).

Delcourt, René, *Expressions d'Argot Allemand et Autrichien* (Paris: De Boccard, 1917).

Dickson, Paul, *War Slang* (Dulles: Brassey's Inc., 1994).

Doyle, Peter and Walker, Julian, *Trench Talk: Words of the First World War* (Stroud: The History Press, 2012).

Esnault, Gaston, *Le Poilu Tel Qu'il Se Parle* (Paris: Éditions Bossard, 1919).

Hochstetter, Gustav, *Der Feldgraue Büchmann* (Berlin: Dr Eysler & Co., 1916).

http://andc.anu.edu.au/australian-words/aif-slang/annotated-glossary.

http://www.bac-lac.gc.ca/eng/discover/
military-heritage/first-world-war/
first-world-war-1914-1918-cef/Pages/
canadian-expeditionary- force.aspx?PHPSESS
ID=07099dsconhg1bbb88djn2i416.

http://www.francetvinfo.fr/societe/guerre-de-
14-18/des-poilus-aux-crapouillots-revisez-l-
argot-de-la-grande-guerre_453240.html.

http://www.wakefieldfhs.org.uk/
War%20Slang.htm.

Jack, Albert, *It's a Wonderful Word* (London:
Arrow, 2008).

Lighter, Jonathan, 'The Slang of the American
Expeditionary Forces in Europe 1917–1919:
An Historical Glossary', *American Speech*
47(1/2), 5–142.

Maier, John, *Deutsche Soldatensprache* (Karlsruhe:
Braunschen Hofbuchdruckerei, 1917).

Moore, Christopher, *Roger, Sausage & Whippet: A Miscellany of Trench Lingo from the Great War* (London: Headline Publishing Group, 2012).

Palmer, Roy, *What a Lovely War!* (London: Michael Joseph Ltd, 1990).

Sainéan, L., *L'Argot des Tranchées* (Paris: De Boccard, 1915).

Warner, Guy, *World War One Aircraft Carrier Pioneer: The Story and Diaries of JM McCleery RNAS RAF* (Barnsley: Pen & Sword, 2011).